When Writing Workshop Isn't Working

{ A N S W E R S
TO TEN TOUGH
Q U E S T I O N S
GRADES 2–5 }

Mark Overmeyer

Mark Overmeyer

Foreword by Stephanie Harvey

 Stenhouse Publishers • Portland, Maine

Stenhouse Publishers
www.stenhouse.com

Library of Congress Cataloging-in-Publication Data
Overmeyer, Mark, 1961–
    When writing workshop isn't working : answers to ten tough questions,
  grades 2–5 / Mark Overmeyer.
        p.   cm.
    Includes bibliographical references.
    ISBN 1-57110-404-6 (alk. paper)
    1. Composition (Language arts)—Study and teaching.
    2. Written communication—Study and teaching.   I. Title.
PN181.O84   2005
372.62'3044—dc22   2005051570

Cover and interior design by Jan Streitburger
Typeset by TNT
Photo by Dennis Molitor

Manufactured in the United States of America on acid-free paper

11   9 8 7 6 5 4

Dedicated to all of the students and teachers
who so generously gave their time
during the writing of this book.

Contents

Foreword

I first met Mark Overmeyer at a kids' theater school on the week of my son Alex's sixth birthday. Alex's coveted birthday present was a summer session where he would begin his lifelong passion for anything theatrical. As we milled about the gaggle of kids, a lanky guy with a wide smile reached his hand out to my somewhat lost and befuddled child and introduced himself as one of the theater teachers. Mark's warm welcome and easy manner spiked instant comfort in my six-year-old son. Alex took to him immediately, only to find out that Mark was teaching older kids that session. "Bummer," Alex murmured. And he was right; for in that moment Alex missed out on one of those once-in-a-lifetime teachers.

Years passed before I ran into Mark again, this time in my role as a staff developer for the Denver-based Public Education and Business Coalition. Mark had signed up to have me come into his sixth-grade classroom to work with his class on writing workshop. I couldn't wait. I still remembered our fleeting introduction years earlier and I knew I was in for a treat working with Mark. As we collaborated on the ins and outs of writing workshop, Mark burst with questions: *How do I help them organize their writ-*

ing? How do I get the most out of conferences? What about kids who won't write? Pressing questions that couldn't be answered definitively in short staff development moments, but rather answered over time with deep thoughtful reflection on kids, writing, teaching, and learning.

Fast-forward ten years to *When Writing Workshop Isn't Working*, the book you hold in your hands. Mark goes beyond merely asking the same questions over and over. Instead, he takes the time to think about the questions, reflect on his kids' learning, and explore solutions. I love the format of this book—the way it's organized around hard, yet common questions that we've all asked ourselves about writing quality, organization, revision, management, planning, and even test writing. Mark understands the need for reflection in his teaching practice. He knows that teachers need to be learners first and he shows us throughout the book that learning is at the heart of his teaching. As we read this book, we see Mark learning along with kids and teachers, trying things out and reflecting on kids' thinking to drive writing instruction. He says it best in the introduction, "It isn't about answers. It is about learning."

And there's much to learn in this book. In chapter after chapter, Mark shares how he has adopted and adapted the tenets of writing workshop to fit the needs of individual kids. He thinks deeply and works hard to solve the questions that pop up when writing workshop gets tough and things don't go the way we had dreamed. So many books on writing make it sound simple. We envision workshops that hum with quiet conversation, buzz with fascinating topics, and sing with writing. But all too often, when we implement workshop, we find too many kids who can't find the right words, struggle with organization, or simply don't want to write. Not all kids hum, buzz, and sing their way through the writing process!

The fact is, teaching kids to write is not that simple. In the 1980s, when writing workshop began to take hold, teachers dramatically increased the amount of time kids spent writing, yet they were sometimes disappointed in the results. Although it is extremely important to give kids plenty of time to write, time alone is not enough to guarantee quality writers. Writers need broad experience with a range of genres, plenty of opportunities to respond, and explicit instruction in crafting strategies. In fact, I believe there is some rocket science in teaching writing and this book helps us navigate some of the rough trajectories. Mark doesn't shy away from the tough questions. He works with teachers and kids to find solutions. This book offers a constellation of possibilities to help our kids write expansively and well.

Throughout the book, Mark shows us the writing teacher as master facilitator. We see Mark as he facilitates purposeful student-to-student talk about writing. When kids spend time talking about their writing and telling their stories to each other, the writing comes to life. We watch how he facilitates the connection between reading and writing by surrounding the kids with rich text reminding them that our best writing teachers are the authors we love and read. We peer in as he facilitates the use of time with a variety of techniques including "Stacking the Deck," a conferring management tool that allows teachers to work with several kids at once, maximizing time but still focusing on individual needs.

This book is a nitty-gritty writing teacher's handbook chockfull of how-to hints and useful writing tips that will facilitate a more effective writing workshop. But it is more than that. It is also a steadfast reminder of the power of reflective teaching and learning. It reminds us that asking the tough questions is at the heart of responsive teaching. Only when we reflect on those questions in relation to our kids' thinking will we make a difference in our kids' writing and ultimately their learning.

—Stephanie Harvey

Acknowledgments

If there is a heaven for book loving teachers, surely it looks exactly like The Bookies Bookstore in Denver, Colorado. Where else can you find stacks of the latest books by Cris Tovani, Stephanie Harvey, Anne Goudvis, Debbie Miller, Lucy Calkins, Ralph Fletcher, Georgia Heard, and Katie Wood Ray? Where else can you hear stories from the owner, Sue Lubeck, about the time she met J. K. Rowling before anybody in America had heard of Harry Potter, and Sue had a hunch she would be big someday? And where else can you find encouragement to write your own book about teaching writing? If you ever find yourself in Denver, stop by The Bookies, say hello to Sue, and buy some books. If you are like me, you may have to buy some extra luggage to get all of your books home. Thanks, Sue, for all your encouragement.

Sue put me in contact with Bill Varner, an editor at Stenhouse, who immediately helped me to shape my ideas into a proposal, and then into this book. He is a writer's dream: he makes my ideas much more clear than they would have been in their initial form, and makes me appear much smarter than I feel most days!

I must thank Leslie Blauman, an extraordinary staff developer and fifth-grade teacher who changed my life when I participated in one of her trainings. A year later, I took over her position as a writing coach/staff developer in my district. I still do not feel qualified to fill her shoes, but feel fortunate to have the opportunity to continue the work she began. She will recognize many ideas from her trainings in the first chapter of this book. Thank you, Leslie!

Cris Tovani and Stephanie Harvey inspired me throughout the writing of this book, even though they may not be aware of it. I know Cris and Stephanie, but we are all so busy we don't see each other often. But, lucky for me, they have wonderful books that I could read when I felt completely overwhelmed by the task at hand. Their books on reading instruction sit, dog-eared and marked up, on my bookshelf, and I refer to them constantly as a teacher. As a writer, they also gave me inspiration as I struggled through the process of completing this book. Georgia Heard's amazing book *Awakening the Heart* also provided inspiration, and thank you, Georgia, for allowing me to use the Six Room Poem idea in this book. It is still my favorite writing experience to use with students.

Rick VanDeWeghe, director of the Denver Writing Project, continues to be a mentor and guide as I take this journey as a writer and teacher. Thanks, Rick, and codirectors Tracy Stegall and Lee Waldman, for an amazing summer in 2003, and for all the support and ideas since.

The generosity of teachers never ceases to amaze me. I am always skeptical of staff developers, and I worried that teachers might think I had gone to the "dark side" when I chose a job that required working with teachers more than students. What a learning experience it has been. I am the lucky one—I get to sit and talk with passionate teachers about what they do best, and I get to observe the amazing results they achieve with students. Thank you to everyone who has opened their classrooms to me, and thank you to the students in your classes as well. You have all helped me to become a much better teacher. Particular thanks to Teolyn Bourbonnie, who allowed me to try many of these ideas with her second graders the year before I began writing this book. Teolyn's flexibility, high expectations, and sense of humor made her the ideal teacher to work with as we tried out some of these ideas. Thanks, T! I also must thank Megan Henry, Chris Hyde, and

Roberta Reed for spending time with me—the results of our talks are in Chapter 10.

Finally, I want to thank my family and friends. Now I know what authors mean when they say you do not write a book in isolation: everyone around you hears about it, whether they want to or not. Dennis, and all of my friends, you heard me alternately get excited about and then quickly moan about writing a book. The idea at first seemed great, and much of the writing itself wasn't terribly painful, but there were days when I felt I could not do it any longer. But you all encouraged me. My brother, Scott, needs to be thanked for allowing me to include a slightly-larger-than-life version of a childhood story in this book, and for continually asking me when my book was coming out. And my mother, Elaine, has always given me the independent spirit to try things I never tried before. Thanks, Mom.

Introduction

The first staff development workshop I remember attending was in the fall of 1985, my second year of teaching. It was the day before students were to come into our classrooms, and I remember being concerned that my room wouldn't be ready. The title of the presentation was "The Writer's Workshop," and this meant nothing to me. I sat near the back of the room, filling out my plan book and my grade book with the names of students I had recently received from the office.

I had to abandon my idea that I would use this time to be more ready when the presenter asked us to write. Write?! I just wanted to get some work done. I wanted a presenter who would just hand out some ideas and let us leave early. But now we were being asked to write, and then to share what we wrote!

How my life changed in that one-hour workshop. I had just heard the most amazing news, news that now seems so full of common sense and is hardly revolutionary, but at the time was a complete turnaround from the way I had been told to teach writing in my college coursework. The revolutionary idea was simply this: the best way to teach students to write is to ask them to write.

To write. Not to complete worksheets. Not to memorize capitalization rules. Not to look up words in the dictionary and copy definitions. But to write.

I forgot all about my room as I left the workshop. I got rid of all my sentence packets, grammar worksheets, and paragraph rules. And I sat down and thought about how I could organize my classroom into a writer's workshop.

I would like to tell you that all was perfect that first year, but of course it wasn't. Many things went wrong. I had trouble with management, I didn't ask students to publish often enough, I always ran out of time for conferences, and when I did confer with students I wasn't sure what to say. Many times I felt completely directionless. But my students did write—and they were passionate about what they wrote. They loved to share their writing, which was not my experience my first year teaching. They loved to talk about their writing, and some students even found ways to improve their writing by examining authors' crafts in the novels we read, even though I was many years away from understanding the importance of looking to authors to learn how to write.

I had begun a journey. My guides were Donald Murray (1985) and Donald Graves (1982), who so eloquently wrote about the writing process in its earliest stages of development. They revolutionized the teaching of writing because they see writing for what it is: a process and a craft that students must wrestle with for themselves in order to improve. Their books remind us that teaching writing is a craft as well, and we must learn right along with our students about what works best. Lucy Calkins (1986), another guide on my journey, continues to produce powerful resources for teacher researchers who want to fill their classrooms with writers, regardless of their age. When I moved from elementary to middle school, Nancie Atwell's book *In the Middle* (1987) convinced me that I did not have to abandon the writer's workshop just because students were older. In fact, Atwell's influence convinced me that our middle school students were desperate to still share their stories through their own voices, and that writing was a way to help them feel that someone was listening. Ralph Fletcher (1992), a poet and writer, served as my guide when I wanted to know more about what writers think about the teaching of writing. His sense of humor reminds me that writing is work, but it should also be a joyous experience in our classroom. Katie Wood Ray's influential *Wondrous Words* (1999) taught me that even our youngest students can use professional writing as a model for their own efforts. Books are artifacts students can continually refer to as they attempt to become better writers.

My journey continues to this day. I have worked as a teacher in grades 2 through 8, and as a staff developer in classrooms from kindergarten through high school, and while I have become a much more confident writing teacher, I still struggle with many parts of the writing workshop. Questions still arise—questions of my own, and questions I am now asked as a staff developer: How should I begin my year? What is the best way to motivate students who don't know what to write? How can I help students get ready for state tests in a workshop setting? How should I assess writing?

This book is organized in a series of questions followed by some suggestions that I hope are practical for your classroom. I don't see the suggestions as definitive answers, for as soon as I feel I have the one answer to solve something as complex as teaching writing, I know it is time to retire. We don't need one-size-fits-all answers, for these lead to formulaic approaches that ignore students' individual needs. It isn't about the answers; it's about learning. In the isolating profession of teaching, we can all learn from each other. I have always loved talking to teachers about what works for them, and I especially love talking to those who know that what works today may need to be adjusted tomorrow because each day is different.

This book is meant to be a springboard for thinking about your writing instruction. I hope some of the ideas work for you and your students, and I hope that you will see how the ideas can be adjusted to fit your specific needs.

More than anything, I hope for you and your students that you can feel what I felt in that workshop back in 1985. The facilitator asked us to write about a memory from our childhoods, and then to share our writing with a partner. I had never shared any of my writing before. I don't remember what I wrote, but I remember my partner laughed. She laughed!

It was the first time in my life I felt like a writer.

So be a writer, and ask your students to join you.

How Do I Begin My Writing Instruction?

What I learned the hard way

I live my life in school years, not calendar years. I feel excitement (and slight trepidation) when the school supply sales begin in midsummer. Even though the ads signal summer's end, they remind me, and all teachers across the country, of what is to come: work, yes, but also the opportunity to meet a new group of students. When our students arrive on the first day of school, they come from many different experiences and backgrounds. I have worked in schools where my class list changed the moment my students walked in the door due to high mobility, and I have also worked in schools where I knew who my students would be before the previous school year ended. In all cases, in the beginning of the year, interest, ability, and enthusiasm for writing varies widely from student to student.

I learned the hard way that when I asked fourth- or fifth-grade students to write about a special memory, or second- or third-grade students to write a few sentences about something they liked to do, I would immediately feel overwhelmed by the work they produced. Some of the students produced fluent, clear paragraphs, others wrote very little, some wrote disconnected thoughts, and, most frightening of all, a few produced nothing. When I picked up these papers, I normally let them sit for a week or two before deciding what to do. I have long believed that instruction must be based on assessment, but, when in the same class I had students producing two or three coherent paragraphs while others produced a blank page, where did I begin? How could I manage such a range of ability and/or interest in writing? My students often mirrored my own frustration, for those who struggled with writing certainly did not feel comfortable producing any kind of volume that first day of school. My message to them, in part, was that volume was good. Think of the struggling student sitting next to the fluent writer—the pencil making its way across the page at your neighbor's desk would be a constant reminder that either you lack confidence in writing or you just plain hate to write.

Writing: Not like other subjects

I believe that writing is different from other subject areas because what students produce can lead a teacher in so many different directions. Students normally arrive on the first day of school with testing data in reading, and if they don't, as in the high-mobility schools I have taught in, the data can be generated fairly quickly with teacher-given tests. Mathematics skills can be determined in a similar manner. Once the student's level is determined, there is a place to begin. But with writing, there are *so many* places to begin. What should a teacher tackle first? Sentence structure? Staying on topic? Clear word choice? Using strong verbs?

My initial instinct, perhaps ingrained in me due to my own early experiences with conventions-based writing instruction, was to focus on skills. I noticed every spelling error, each run-on sentence, and the misuse of capital letters. I didn't often notice anything about student work beyond technical errors, and this caused me to be even more overwhelmed. Grammar and skill packets were easy to reproduce, and I used much of my writing time helping students to complete these exercises. Of course, this did not improve their writing skills, nor did it make them want to write. Each year seemed to begin with this same vicious cycle: I asked them to write, I was discouraged by what they wrote, we focused on skills, and then I was still discouraged by what they wrote.

Some basic structures to ensure success

Because I was determined to avoid the same mistake year after year, I now begin my school year in a much more focused manner so that neither my students nor I feel overwhelmed. My first goal is to ensure that all students leave school the first day feeling as if they can produce a short piece of writing and improve upon it. I do not expect them all to love writing, though that would be nice. And, I have also abandoned the idea that if students are simply allowed to write what they want to write, they will enjoy writing and they will eventually improve. This method has never produced strong writing from many of my students. Struggling writers do not like to write anyway, and choice alone does not help them improve in any concrete, structured way. Advanced students tend to want to write stories, or sequels to books they love. This is fine, but often even the strongest writer cannot control fiction for sustained periods of time. I believe strongly that both beginning and advanced writers benefit from having some structures within the writing-process classroom.

These structures are not meant to limit, but merely to focus. Many books written by professional writers give suggested exercises for getting words on the page. Some of these suggestions are very open-ended, and others identify a specific topic to write about. In my work with the National Writing Project in Denver, we often began our day with an open-ended topic: Write for five minutes about something that you fear. Tell about a time you were proud of an accomplishment. Write about your favorite food.

These suggested topics provided a structure that freed me to write. If we had entered the room each day and had been told to write whatever we wanted, I would have struggled. The suggested topics provided an idea, and our discussions about our writing were much more focused because everyone had a unique perspective on each topic. When I reflect on my own experiences as a writer, I realize that I had choice, even when given a topic to write about. I could choose which fear to focus on, which proud accomplishment to relate, which food to describe using sensory details. When I ask students to write about a particular topic or when I give them an idea, I still focus my instruction on the importance of choice. I tell them that writers always make choices, both in what to write and how to write it. My goal is to empower them, and to help them understand how they can use their choices in a newly formed community of writers. This use of topics to encourage writing helps to structure and limit the wide range of styles of writing students might produce. It helps because writing seems smaller, and doable—not unimportant, certainly not insignificant, but manageable.

So—where to begin?

Start small

I walked into my room an hour before school started on the first day of school last year and found the name-tags of my new students on top of my desk. I placed them randomly on desks, trying to have at least two girls and two boys at each table grouping. This ritual calmed and excited me: here were my new students' names, and each tag represented someone who was getting ready to come to school in an hour! I placed a clean sheet of lined paper and a sharpened pencil on each desk. I set my copy of *Owl Moon* on my reading chair, wrote my name on the chalkboard, and felt ready to take on the challenges of the new year.

Based on suggestions from a very talented teacher I had the honor of working with during my first year of teaching, I have always done something academic, yet interesting, as a starter the first day of school. Though students love their supplies and enjoy getting organized, this mentor teacher reminded me that kids like to learn. Setting the tone with a positive writing experience seems to be the perfect way to start the school year.

I greeted my students at the door when the bell rang. After spending some time getting to know each other, I sat in the reading chair and students joined me on the floor.

"This is a book you may know, and that's great," I began, holding up *Owl Moon*. "Today we are going to read it to help us form some ideas for writing. This is a memory book. It's about an unforgettable moment in a child's life when she went looking for owls with her father. No matter how many times I read the book, I am amazed at how Jane Yolen can create such interesting writing about looking for an owl."

After reading the book, I asked students to think of a moment in their lives they would never forget.

"Think of a perfect day. What did you do? Who were you with? Think of as many details as you can about a perfect day. If you cannot think of a perfect day you have experienced, then describe a day that would be perfect."

Hands went up to share.

"One of my perfect days was at the beach in Hawaii," Hannah shared.

"All of my favorite days start with pancakes!" Matt laughed, and was soon joined by other students who thought of food.

"Can we write about sports?" asked Katherine.

"Of course," I said.

"Good—because I shot the winning goal when our soccer team went to regionals last year."

"I can't wait to read about it!" I told her.

I listed general topics on the board based on our discussion:

Food
Sports
Vacations
Friends
Birthdays

I explained to students that we were going to write about our experiences. I cautioned them not to list details about every part of their perfect day, but encouraged them to think of one particular moment. I referred to Jane Yolen's text and encouraged them to remember what she did as she wrote: she slowed down and highlighted key moments in the day. This technique, which I have now used in many classrooms, grades K through 6, helps to create an environment in which writing is seen as manageable, and yet full of choice. Even though I typically ask students to write about a perfect day or a perfect moment, my intent is to allow choice within structure. Students choose their own moments. I am helping them to focus their writing into something they can contain, something small yet important they do not want to forget.

To help students make their experience more concrete I decided to act out a moment in one of my most memorable days. I asked for volunteers to act out my story about going with three friends to a water park when I was young. I quickly chose some students, and then asked them to come to the front of the room. As I placed the students in their positions on the "stage," I

Making the experience concrete before writing

began my story about my day at the water park, and focused only on my fear of heights while I climbed the tallest water slide in the park. I encouraged the actors playing me and my friends to talk as kids do—to laugh, and to tease me when I showed my fear on the slide.

"The best part of that day was finally landing in the water after I went down the slide. I was so relieved it was over. Now, when you write today, I want you to think about a moment in your perfect day you can describe. Make a movie in your mind. Think of the details. I am going to write a model sentence on the board about my day, which may help you think of a way to start your stories. It's an idea if you get stuck."

I wrote on the board:

> I was having a perfect day at the swimming pool, but then my friend Susan suggested we go on the biggest slide in the park.

"I am trying to make the reader interested in my story immediately when I write this. I jump right into the story. When you acted it out for me, it helped me to remember some of the details. Are you ready to write?"

My students headed back to their seats, and began describing their perfect days. Though some students took some individual prompting and coaching to start their stories, the acting seemed to motivate them to put their ideas on paper.

As I mentioned before, if students turn in a blank paper, nothing is more frightening for a writing teacher. To minimize the chance of this happening, I always ask students who feel they have nothing to write about to wait with me on the floor while everyone else begins

What about the reluctant writers?

writing at their seats. I then talk with this small group in more detail about some experiences I have had that may help them. Mentioning a birthday party, or a favorite food, often helps to spark an idea. I was in a kindergarten class recently when the teacher and I mentioned how much we love popcorn, and before we knew it every hand was in the air, students eager to share their stories about eating popcorn at the movies with their grandparents or at home with their families. Food has a way of bringing forth memories. With this small group, I will often write a more generic opening lead sentence to get them started:

> I woke up and knew it would be a perfect day because I could smell pancakes cooking on the griddle.

Most students can manage to write a few sentences about what they would eat for breakfast on a perfect day.

I make it very clear to all students that they can begin their writing in any way they choose to honor those who are more confident, but I leave my suggestions on the board.

I walk around the room for a few minutes, and if some students aren't writing, I ask them to copy the sentence about food so that they can at least get something on the page. I made a deal with one of my fifth-grade students two years ago on the first day of school: if I wrote a sentence, he would write one. The first day, his entire piece was two sentences long. By the fourth or fifth day, his pieces were four sentences long: two sentences written by each of us. At the end of the first month of school, he was writing five to six sentences on his own. I told him I would never ask him to recopy during the first few weeks of school, that I would not focus on mistakes, and that we would work through his reluctance to write together. By limiting his stress, I was convincing this student that he could rely on my assistance, and before long, he knew he could write on his own.

I monitor student progress for approximately five minutes once writing time has begun this first day, or until everyone in my fourth- or fifth-grade classes has three to five sentences, and everyone in my second- or third-grade classes has two sentences. If more than ten minutes go by, I just make sure that everyone has one original sentence. The reason I limit the time is because I want students to build capacity. I don't want my struggling writers to feel that writing time is endless, and I don't want my advanced writers to write two or three pages, and then feel that they always finish, and are left waiting because some students struggle. I try to avoid hearing "I'm done!" during the writing block. When I ask students to find a place to stop, I tell them clearly I didn't expect them to finish. I give them two warnings. In a quiet voice I say:

> "I am going to ask you to find a place to stop in about two minutes. Don't worry about getting done. I don't expect you to finish."

Then, about a minute and a half later I say:

> "Please find a place to stop. If you haven't finished the sentence you are on, find a good place to stop. Please put your pencils down so that I know you are finished."

Revising through identifying the qualities of good writing

After students have completed a draft of a memoir/small moment in their writer's notebook, I ask a few students to share their work. The other students listen for strong moments in the story they hear, and identify these moments specifically.

In Liz Nelson's and Jackie Alden's fifth-grade classes, everyone has finished at least half of a small moment story, and Liz's student Olivia shares her piece about the time her mother asked her to help her younger brother put on his socks. Her story is full of imagery and has a clear sense of story and purpose.

"The Feet" by Olivia

"Olivia, go tie your brother's shoes!" "Oh mom, do I have to?" "Yes." You're wondering why I dread tying my brother's shoes? Well here's your answer. It was a fine morning, we were all dressed our best for school. In my mom's case work. I was in my parent's bedroom awaiting for my mom to do my hair. "Olivia," she said, "can you tie your brother's shoes?" I gave her a swift nod and skipped to my brother's room. I saw him sitting in the middle of the floor, with his innocent face, spit bubbles, and he was charging his socks at each other. I went to his shoe box. I called to my mom, "Which shoes should he put on?" "The white ones," she replied. There were two pairs of white shoes. I just snatched the ones that looked better. I took my brother's socks from him. Then, I picked up a foot, and PU WEA. I gagged and shook my head. I hastily put on his socks, shoes, and tied his shoes. After that, I ran out the door. Well, there you have it. I will never tie my brother's shoes again. Plus, I'm just plain lazy.

When I ask what students notice about the piece, Jane says: "She has vivid verbs."

This one statement tells me that the students have been engaged in prior conversations about good writing.

"Which verbs?" I ask.

"Like gagged," she responds.

Clearly, this student is familiar with the idea that strong verbs help to create good writing.

Brandon says of Olivia's piece: "She has good details."

"Which details do you remember?" I probe.

"I don't know—she just makes a picture in your head."

"Can you tell us about a picture you have from the story?"

He is unable to think of a specific example, so I open it up to the group:

"How many of you think Olivia did a good job of creating a picture in our minds?"

Many students raise their hands.

"Can you tell me one place where Olivia made a picture in your mind?"

Vivian responds, "She said her brother had spit bubbles coming out of his mouth."

"Good! That makes a great picture! It helps us to see her brother, and to understand that he is very young."

This type of work isn't time-consuming, but is most helpful when it is very directed and specific. I list the qualities mentioned on the board:

- vivid verbs (gagged)
- makes a picture in our heads (spit bubbles)

I then challenge the class to find similar or new qualities of good writing in the first page of *Owl Moon*.

From a five-minute discussion of this wonderfully written small moment, we add the following qualities to the list:

- similes (comparing two things)
- hearing words
- seeing words
- time words (winter, night, long past bedtime)

This list becomes a toolbox for revision. I place a copy of my own personal narrative on the overhead, a childhood tale of getting in trouble for pulling all the roses off a rosebush when I was supposed to be weeding the roses with my friends. I ask students to help me find one place to improve the story. Many hands go up. Jason thinks I should add a simile in the section about the last rose my friends and I are about to pick off a rose bush:

"You could say the rose bush looks as bare as—"

He stops, and I wait.

"What could be bare?" I ask after about thirty seconds.

He shrugs.

"Do you want to think for a minute, or do you want some help?"

He chooses to get help from someone, so I open it up to the group. After some discussion, we all agree to the following:

The bush looked as sad as a dog who lost his owner.

I write this revision on my piece in color, and ask students to choose a color (other than red) to make their revisions.

"I want to see where you changed your minds, and I want you to know that it is perfectly fine to change your mind. If you erase, you have no record of how you are growing as a writer. You may also want to go back and change something to its original form."

I remind students to look at the list of writing qualities we noticed in Olivia's piece and *Owl Moon*. "These are some ways we can improve our writing. These are the things we like about the good writing we have noticed today." During revision, I time the students for five minutes, trying to make it around the room to make sure that everyone makes at least one revision. Then we stop.

"Writers, please stop! How long did you work?"

"A few minutes," one boy says.

"Exactly. So, when we revise, we can make some decisions about improving our writing very quickly. To make an entire piece better, you need to take more time. But for practice, you can make a piece better by making just one or two changes. I am not asking you to change the whole piece, but just to make it better. Raise your hands if you think you made your piece better today."

If I have watched the class carefully during the revision time to make sure that everyone has made at least one improvement, I typically get every student in the class to raise their hands. I do not want students to think of writing as easy so much as something they *can do*. I also want them to think of revision as something that writers do as a matter of course, not always something that waits until the end of a writing experience. And most of all, I do not want students to equate revision with recopying.

Here are some revisions Olivia made in her story:

- She added the following line after her mother told her she had to tie her brother's shoes:
  "Although I love my brother, the objects that lay under his ankles are another story."
- After the section about waiting for her mother to do her hair, she added:
  "I entered the room and plopped on the cloud-like bed. My mom was in the bathroom doing my sister's hair."
- And this simile about the smell of her brother's feet:
  "His feet stunk as awful as ten-thousand garbage trucks. Maybe even worse."

The last part is key to the success of a writing program. I tell my students from the very first day that our writing will be shared. This is key because your students write like students—you don't. Professional, adult writing can be used as a model for student writing, but students in a class need to hear what students their own age are writing. They need to discuss their writing process. When I ask students to share, I often ask

The importance of sharing

them to explain how they thought of their ideas, why they chose a particular word, or how they organized their thoughts before they wrote. Sometimes, the answers are vague, but, as students become accustomed to having these discussions, they share good advice for all the writers in the classroom. And, since everyone shares something early on in the year, they understand that not only the strong writers can give advice. Some of the best writing advice in my classroom has come from struggling writers.

The way I make sure that every student in the class shares something is simple: if there are 24 students in my class, I have 8 students share something after the first short writing time, 8 different students share after revising by adding a detail or two, and the remaining 8 students' work I take home, find excerpts that can be used as examples of strong, detailed writing, and use these as discussion starters for the next day's class. If students are uncomfortable sharing their writing, I let them know that I would be happy to share it. If they decline, I share theirs anonymously as part of the third group of 8 mentioned above. When the importance of sharing writing is introduced the first day of school, I find little resistance from students because they see it as a norm in the classroom.

Students who have not mastered English

English Language Learners are becoming a larger part of many school populations across the country. When language is a barrier, it is important to use different strategies to make directions clear. If writing involves some kind of personal memory, the acting idea mentioned above can help ELL students to understand that we are writing stories about our lives. When students share ideas for stories prior to writing, their memories can also be acted out, or drawn in a series of three or four quick sketches on the chalkboard. Sketches provide an opportunity to discuss the sequence of events in a memory story. Picture books with clear, sequenced pictures, like those in *Owl Moon*, also help students who do not speak English.

If ELL students are literate in their own language, I ask them to write about a memory in their own language. If the students are not literate in their own language, I ask them to draw a sequence of pictures. I have had success with this method, with the help of the picture books, acting, and demonstrating how a sequence of sketches can tell a story. Once pictures are drawn, vocabulary can be introduced as you help the English learner to label the pictures. Even if a child is monolingual, I believe it is key to include all children in the processes of the writing classroom. We learn through observation, and by welcoming all students to be part of our daily rituals, we will more quickly help them to attain the language they need to succeed.

Last year in a first-grade classroom, Anfal had just moved to America not long before I visited the class. She spoke very little English. After sharing *Owl Moon*, acting out my story about fear of heights at a water park, and sketching my story as a model, Anfal drew and labeled herself outside a pool, inside a pool with a smile on her face (the drawing was labeled), and then inside the pool with a frown.

I pointed to the third picture.

"What happened here? Why are you sad?"

Anfal didn't understand.

"Were you sad?"

I traced over the sad face on the drawing.

She nodded.

"Cold," she whispered.

I helped Anfal construct a simple sentence for each picture.

Anfal had to learn more English before she could really add life to her story, but she had enough basic words that she could join the class by constructing a story in a way that made sense to her. I think the visual images from the picture book, the acting, and modeling of my own sketches as I wrote a model story helped Anfal succeed in telling a story from her life.

Other ideas for the beginning of the year

In addition to asking students to write about something from their own life based on a picture book, here are some other ideas for motivating similar writing early in the school year:

- Ask students to bring in objects or artifacts that represent an important moment in their lives. They might bring in photos, or trophies, or a special gift from a friend or relative. As the teacher, you should bring in similar artifacts. Students can share their objects in small groups, and with feedback from their group, write the story of why one object is important to them. This idea lends itself to descriptive writing as well.

- Use video clips from a film to inspire writing. A short clip from a film provides an immediate visual image for students to draw upon as they think of their own experiences. Cartoon films such as *Monsters, Inc.*, *Finding Nemo*, and *Toy Story* all have scenes that examine themes of friendship, family, and how to deal with fears. These clips can lead to class discussions about stories in our own lives. Live action films such as *Home Alone*, *The Sandlot*, and *A Christmas Story* can also provide inspiration for students to tell their own stories.

- If it is more motivating for students to write fictional narratives rather than personal narratives earlier in the year, I have used the film clip idea mentioned above, as well as excerpts from books and a section from a picture book to motivate writing. Short animated films can provide wonderful fodder for story ideas. The British claymation films featuring Wallace and Gromit are wonderful inspirations for stories. You can show a clip from the beginning of one of their short films, and then ask students to fill in the rest of the story. If students are ready for a challenge immediately, a three- to five-minute clip from the middle of a film can be shown, and then students can write their own beginning and ending. One feature of the Wallace and Gromit films (easily found in video stores) is that there is very little language. The stories are visual, and ELL students will understand the narratives as clearly as English speakers. They are also appropriate for all ages. Picture books with a strong narrative can be used in a similar manner, with students filling in either the beginning, middle, or end of stories after you share an excerpt. If I use text in a similar fashion, I have had more success if I make it into a reader's theater experience. For example, I might use a chapter from Louis Sachar's wonderful *Sideways Stories from Wayside School*, and rewrite it as a script. His book is full of many short, slightly off-kilter tales of a school built thirty stories tall. Each story of the school is a classroom, and the tales are full of multiple characters and very funny dialogue. Even though many students are familiar with this book, I have had great success in using the tales to encourage students to develop their own ideas for stories. If these tales are too complex, the classic *Frog and Toad* tales of Arnold Loebel can be used for second- or third-grade writers in a similar fashion.

Final thoughts

I cannot claim that the methods described above solve the difficulties inherent in writing instruction. I still have many needs I must address, and I still end my day realizing the task is formidable. But, I feel successful if students have produced writing, begun a discussion about the qualities of good writing, and already revised their writing, even if in the most basic way. I want students to understand from the first day of school that writing is indeed a process, and that it is one we will engage in throughout the year. And by starting with something that motivates them to write and to care about what they have written, I begin the year energized, ready to help my students grow as writers and thinkers.

{ CHAPTER }
2

How Can I Help Students Who Don't Know What to Write About?

Focus on what students know

Writers often give the advice to write what you know. This sounds deceptively simple until it is tried. What *do* we know? The obvious place to begin is with our own lives, and yet the genre of memoir tends to have a fondness for looking back on childhood that students cannot always grasp because they are still living the lives so many authors use as fodder for their poems, stories, and novels. The key is to guide students to write specifically in the genre of memoir by looking for stories in their own lives.

When students are asked to write about themselves, they may say nothing ever happens to them, or they still cannot think of anything to write about. Part of the problem may come

Make a list

from the teacher's directions. If students are asked to write about their summer, or their favorite vacation, or even a birthday party, the problem is not that there is not enough to write about, but that there is too much. Even a birthday party has many stories: Who was there? Was it a surprise party? Were there presents? Did you get what you wanted? What kind of food did you have? What kind of cake? What rituals does your family have concerning birthdays?

Helping students to focus their memoirs is a way to begin to tackle the huge subject of life. The key is specificity. One way to help this along is to ask students for a title to their piece before they begin to write. If they say "Summer vacation," for example, then you know the writing will be impossible to control. Even the title "Swimming" can be too general. A better title would be: "Getting in trouble for swimming" or "The scary water slide." These last titles refer to specific moments, rather than large blocks of time. I often ask students to think of a story that happened in less than five minutes. When they think in these terms, then real stories emerge, and they can control their writing more effectively.

As these stories emerge and become clear, they can become the resource for lists of what students can write about. Although the list can be lengthy, it is more useful to students than a list that is more general. Some example lists of specific memoir ideas are listed below, from Jonathan Pacic's fifth-grade classroom:

Pets
begging for a pet
pets biting/scratching/barking
runaway pets
pets digging holes in the yard
a hurt pet
sick pets
a new pet

Family and friends
mean brothers/sisters
helpful brothers/sisters
chores
arguing

teasing
playing sports/games
sleepovers
getting in trouble

Holidays/birthdays/celebrations
weddings
Fourth of July
Halloween
Christmas
Hanukkah
surprise parties
Valentine's Day

The length of the list is determined by the needs of the students. Once a good list is developed, it can be typed and reproduced and given to students for a continual resource and a reminder that all students have stories they can tell from their lives.

Prior to writing stories, an effective method for helping students to tell their stories is to ask them to interview each other. Begin by modeling this process.

Use the interview

Ask a student or another teacher, if available, to be your partner, and then tell a story. It works best if you tell your partner to stop you if you are *not* telling a story, but just giving you a list of events that happened. I typically will purposely do this, because one of the characteristics of many students' writing in grades 2 through 5 is that it resembles a list:

> I had a surprise birthday party. My parents surprised me. We played games. We opened presents. We ate cake.

I begin with my partner in a similar way:

> My brother and I always got in trouble. My mom would get mad at us. She would tell us to go to our rooms. We couldn't play.

If you recite this kind of story, your partner (or someone from the class) should stop you because you are creating a list rather than telling a story. This non-example should prevent at least some of the students from falling into the same listing trap.

Once you tell your story, ask your partner to identify whether or not it was a story, and why. Then, ask your partner to tell a story, and you listen. Stop your partner if he or she doesn't tell a story. When the class works together with partners, I time each partner for one minute. I ask them to try to stretch their small moment story into one minute or more. If they don't finish at the one-minute mark, I tell them this is a good thing: it means they have a lot to write about.

This method of oral rehearsal can help many students who are stuck, and it also allows all writers in the class to get a sense of their story and to rehearse it before they put it on paper. As students begin to write, if there are still students who don't have a story, I meet with them and ask them questions. Here are some questions that have worked for me in the past, and generally get some kind of story:

Do you have a pet?
If yes:
> Can you tell me a story about something funny your pet did? (I avoid stories about pets dying for small-moment stories, because they generally should become longer narratives, or a string of several narratives.)

If no:
> Can you tell me a story about asking your parents to get a pet?
>
> Can you tell me a story about something funny one of your friend's pets did?

Do you have a brother or sister?
If yes:
> Can you tell me a story about a time when you argued with your brother or sister?
>
> Can you tell me a story about a time when you helped your brother or sister, or when they helped you?

What is your favorite food?
After response:
> Can you complete this idea?
> One time we were eating _____ and _____.

Here is a sample exchange with a second-grade student who was stuck after the interview with her partner. She wanted to write about a birthday party, but she didn't know what to focus on:

"Was it your birthday?" I ask.

"Yes," Jane responds.

Because I didn't want to encourage a list-like story, I immediately tried to find a story within a story. I avoided questions about favorite gifts, or who came to the party:

"Did anything funny happen at the party?"

Jane thought for a minute.

"I snuck into the kitchen before the party to see my cake."

"What? You did? What happened? Did you get caught?"

"My mom came in and saw me."

"Uh-oh! What did she do?"

"She came over and took some frosting off the cake and licked it off her finger," Jane laughed.

"No way! And did you try some frosting too?"

"Yes."

"Then what happened?"

"My aunt came in and caught us. She ate some frosting too."

"So what happened when the party started?"

"Everybody noticed some of the frosting was missing, but we never told."

"That's a great story! You could write some great details about when your mom caught you looking at your cake. How did you feel?"

"I was worried she would be mad. But she wasn't."

"How did you feel when she licked the frosting?"

"I was so surprised! We laughed."

"So, do you think you could write your story now?"

"Yes."

Jane headed back to her seat, ready to write. A focused conversation can often help students when they are uncertain about what to write. The use of verbal rehearsal in the form of an interview has helped many of my students over the years become more confident writers.

Use mentor texts

Many children's authors write memoir very effectively. The most effective titles I have used to model the idea that stories come from very small moments include *Owl Moon* by Jane Yolen and *Fireflies* by Julie Brinckloe. Both of these books are deceptively simple. Before I introduce *Fireflies*, I tell students that Brinckloe could have written the entire book in one sentence: I saw a bunch of fireflies and caught them and then let them go. I then ask them to listen carefully to see how the author stretches the story to make it interesting for the reader. *Owl Moon* and *Fireflies* help students to see that they have stories in their own lives, and that they can begin looking for small moments to write about.

One way to convince students they can write effective memoirs, and even enjoy it, is to maximize the chances for success during short mini-lessons. Think of an experience you can share that may resonate with the students in your class. I often tell a story about taking care of my friend's cat, Milo. Milo stayed at my apartment, and one day when I went home I couldn't find him. I had done laundry early in the morning in the laundry room down the hall, and I worried that he had gotten out and I didn't notice. I describe looking for him everywhere, and then finally discovering him playing with the soap in the bathtub. This moment works well as a story because I can add many details about looking for the cat, and I can describe my feelings of worry and relief. The texts mentioned above, *Owl Moon* and *Fireflies*, are gently emotional pieces that I have found students can identify with. I intentionally avoid big moments: weddings attended, birth of a brother or sister, or a death. These are very appropriate for memoir, but for helping all students to feel they have something to say in a short amount of time, these topics tend to be too large.

After sharing my story, I ask students for some title ideas. "Missing Milo" or "Where's the Cat?" work better as titles than "The Cat" because they help to limit the time frame to just a few minutes. I ask students to think about a story they might write about, and then to share titles. Putting a few of these titles on the board is normally enough to get everyone started, and then I let students write.

Below is a sample of some titles for small moment stories from different grade level groups:

- "Where'd She Go?"—
  a fifth grader's story about losing her sister when she was supposed to be baby sitting
- "Scavenger Hunt"—
  a fifth grader's story about cleaning up after the dog in the backyard.
- "Frosting Trouble"—
  a second grader's story about licking all the frosting off the cake at her birthday party

Sometimes, students want to tell your story instead of focusing on their own. I have worked in many classrooms, and unless I am very specific, I can receive four or five stories about trying to find a pet cat, and invariably the cat ends up being in the bathtub, playing with the soap. I tell students that they can tell a story about a pet, but they must focus on a different set of details.

"Your story cannot be about finding your pet cat in the bathtub," I tell them, "even if this really happened. Think of something else you can tell me about your cat."

Below is a story by Dorion, a third-grade student at Sunrise Elementary:

> Once I had a cat and I took the cat food out of the cabinet and took the cookies out of the pot and I put the cat food in the pot and the cat had the cookies. Then my brother Michael asked my mom if he could have a cookie. And my mom said yes. And my brother reached into the pot and he said mom the cookies are all mushy something went wrong. And took some out and ate it and he said it was bad and it tasted like kitty food.

Dorion's story is about something that happened in just a few minutes. He writes with detail from the very beginning, and the ending we anticipated makes us laugh when we get there. Dorion was successful because he chose a moment in his life that he remembers, and he is able to create a story from it.

Not all successful writing experiences have to come from students' lives. I have used many different writing activities over the years to spark student interest and confidence in writing.

Develop anchor writing experiences

When I reflect on my writing instruction over the years, I realize that I do not always frame writing in a positive light. I have many stories about how difficult writing is, or about how my teachers used to mark my papers with red pens. While finishing my master's degree, I often told students about the painful process of writing my thesis. These stories do not create a positive feeling for writing in students' minds, and when I compare these stories to my many stories about loving books and reading, I realize I need to consider how to frame writing in the same positive light as reading.

Anchor writing activities have served me well in the past few years. I have typically used anchor texts in my reading class: whether a read-aloud such as *Because of Winn-Dixie* or the class novel *Holes*, I had books, poems, and stories I could refer to throughout the year as instructional guides and examples of positive reading experiences. I needed to do the same for writing. One answer came in the form of the RAFT.

RAFT is an acronym for **R**ole **A**udience **F**ormat **T**opic, an idea developed by Carol Santa. RAFTs are often used while writing in the content areas, as Janet Allen describes in her book *Tools for Teaching Content Literacy*. When composing a RAFT, the writer must keep each of the components in mind. The best way to explain a RAFT is with an example:

RAFTs

> Imagine you are a turkey (**R**ole) writing to a farmer (**A**udience) in the form of a letter (**F**ormat) and you are begging the farmer to choose some other turkey for Thanksgiving dinner (**T**opic).

Below is a sample RAFT using the details listed above:

> Dear Farmer Bob: November 20, 2002
>   I understand you are about to choose a turkey for this year's feast. Well, you can pass right by my coop. I have been really sick—chicken pox! Those chickens came to visit us last week to brag about being safe for awhile this month, and before you know it, I got sick. You certainly do not want your family to catch this disease, so choose another turkey. I think Sam in coop 5 looks healthy and fat this year. I am losing weight daily, so I could never feed you and your wife and kids. Maybe next year . . .
>   Your friend,
>   Turkey

Students can be given an example of a RAFT such as this one, or they can be introduced to RAFTs through picture books. *Dear Mrs. LaRue* and *Detective LaRue* by Mark Teague are excellent examples of RAFTs. They detail the woes of a dog who feels he has been wrongly sent to obedience school, and then is accused of being the reason for a pair of missing cats. The format of each book is a series of letters written by the dog, with a very distinct perspective about how he is being treated. The books are humorous and full of voice.

In a fourth-grade class at Sunrise Elementary, Ms. Cimino's students were enthusiastic about trying out their own RAFTs after hearing *Dear Mrs. LaRue*. They brainstormed some ideas for RAFTs first, mostly focusing on pets who were either angry at their owners, or jealous of other pets in the house. Some of their ideas are listed below:

Role	Audience	Format	Topic
Tiger	Antelope	Letter	I'm going to eat you!
Antelope	Tiger	Letter	You can't catch me!
Bird	Cat	Story	Bird teases cat about flying

After brainstorming several ideas, we decided that the best way to practice the RAFT would be to write a letter. Students enthusiastically responded to the challenge of writing from a different perspective.

Jessica wrote an imaginary letter from a mouse to a cat:

> Dear Susan the Cat,
> I can fit into more places than you. But I thought I'd be nice and give you some advice. The only way you'll be able to fit into as many places as I can is by not eating for one week, not chasing me, and not talking to any other cats. After the one week passes come meet me by the old oak tree. I will give you a test and see if you followed all of my directions. You better meet me!
> Sincerely,
> Paul the Mouse

RAFTs can be used as an anchor assignment in many ways. Students can brainstorm RAFTs with a month theme. For example, they may want to write about the leaves falling in October from many perspectives, or about Halloween. Many months have holidays that lend themselves to RAFT topics, and other months can focus on seasonal, weather-related RAFTs. Pictures can also be used to generate RAFT ideas: students can examine photos from sports magazines, or pictures of places in postcards.

For the past several years, RAFTs have provided many of my students with a very positive attitude toward writing. Because this anchoring activity was almost universally loved by the students, the writing time became more positive. The open-ended creativity within the structure provided by the RAFT allows students of all writing abilities to feel successful.

Writing across the curriculum

Students who do not like to create their own stories or memoirs may be more motivated to write when presented with interesting facts found in social studies or science. Writing does not need to be confined to the language arts block, and the writing in social studies and science does not need to be confined to formulaic, predictable assignments.

When students are motivated by a topic in another subject area, it is the perfect time to capitalize on this interest. Students in all grades love facts about many different topics, typically beginning with dinosaurs in the primary grades. It is amazing to sit and listen to students talk about the tiniest details regarding the history's largest creatures. Kids remember facts about animals, places, video games, and sports—so we need to tap into their natural curiosity when we are considering topics for writing.

Since a fascination with animals is nearly universal across gender and age lines, using the topic of animals for writing has some strong possibilities.

If you want to focus on description, postcards, calendars on sale at the beginning of the year, and even video clips can be helpful. Students can be asked to describe the movements and/or habits of animals in these photos or clips. As they become more adept at description, while the writer shares, other students in the class can guess what animal is being described.

Gathered animal facts can be turned into poems or descriptive paragraphs. Students can use animal facts to generate RAFT ideas, as mentioned above. Facts about other topics can be used as well, but animals do tend to be a popular topic for students of all ages.

Guess Which Picture

A very successful writing experience I have used with grades 1 through 6 involves asking students to describe what they see in a photo or painting. Calendar pictures work well for this. I hand out photos of landscapes, city scenes, or sporting events and ask students to describe what they see. Typically, I will ask students to work with a partner on this activity. Students spread around the room and they do not let anyone else see what picture they are working on. After everyone has about twenty minutes to write descriptively in pairs about what they see in their photos, I put the pictures on the chalkboard with magnets or tape. Each picture is assigned a number. When student pairs share their writing, the rest of the students guess which picture they are describing. This writing experience gives the writer a sense of audience, and it also gives the audience a reason to listen to each writer. As students share their work, we talk about the elements of descriptive writing included in each piece.

I have worked in many classrooms with ELL students using the anchor writing experiences described. If a class or teacher model is presented for each type of writing prior to asking students to write, then all students tend to be more successful. This model writing

ELL students and anchor writing activities

can serve as a place to find vocabulary for a word bank that ELL students can use. Each of the activities involves a visual component as well: students can either draw pictures and then label them to relate their own experiences, and they can use visual cues in the Guess Which Picture activity.

These anchor activities can provide ELL students with the opportunity to succeed at their own level, and they are meant to be repeated, so when the activities are used a second or third time, ELL students will become more clear about what is expected. They will have more language to relate their experiences and to describe their world.

Final thoughts

The ideas mentioned in this section attempt to move beyond just one genre of writing. If I am working on a memoir unit in the beginning of the year, my focus is to ask students to write stories about themselves. But, if they have trouble producing much writing even when I provide visual cues, acting opportunities, and other motivators for developing story ideas, I need to branch out. My belief is that once students produce something they are excited to share, then they start to see themselves as writers. The RAFT idea has convinced some of my most reluctant writers that they, too, have ideas, and lessons that involve acting help some students become "unstuck." Once writing is produced, I can lead students in a discussion about what we notice about the writing they are creating, and then I can incorporate these ideas into any unit of study. The picture guessing idea lends itself to a discussion about descriptive writing, and then students can incorporate their knowledge of imagery and figurative language into the unit we are working on at the time. My goal in using an anchor activity is to include all students in the community of writers, and to help them join in the discussion of what writers do. If I can accomplish this, then I can refer to a successful anchor writing experience in order to help students who feel less successful with writing.

{ C H A P T E R }
3

How Can I Help My Students Develop Better Vocabulary and Word Choice?

Working with elementary school students' writing provides unique challenges in regard to vocabulary. Some students overuse new vocabulary terms. In a second-grade classroom I recently visited, I read aloud a book about an octopus, and the giant sea animal was described as "jetting" through the water. Many students immediately latched onto this strong verb, and soon, in every piece these students wrote, "jetting" became the verb of choice. I read stories about students jetting home from school, jetting to the playground, and jetting down the road with their parents in the car.

Students in elementary school often overuse the thesaurus as well. I was working with a group of fifth graders on using sensory details as a way to help make pictures in the readers' minds, and we were crafting a sentence about riding on a roller coaster.

When I asked them to add stronger word choice to the sentence "I screamed when I went on the roller coaster," a student immediately piped in with, "I uttered loudly when I went on the roller coaster!" We worked together to try and craft a more accurate sentence, while being sensitive to the new idea. My journey toward helping students develop ideas for stronger word choice has been a long one, and I am convinced that one of the best methods of helping students to create stronger writing is to read like writers.

Teach students to read like writers

Much has been written about helping students to read like writers. Katie Wood Ray's wonderful guide to this approach, *Wondrous Words,* is an invaluable resource for any teacher who wants to learn more about how to help young writers use authors as mentors. I think that the idea of using mentor texts is valuable for all writers, and some of my favorite lessons involve students examining the craft of writers like Jane Yolen and Cynthia Rylant.

I think this work can be done with student writing as well. Students can examine their own work to find examples of strong, descriptive language and words that invite readers into the text. The most effective strategy I have used for creating strong student writing is to teach the class about "showing writing." As described in Ken Macrorie's book *Telling Writing,* showing writing is descriptive and "telling writing" is statement driven:

> She was excited.

Showing writing is driven by images, and therefore creates a clear picture in the reader's mind:

> She jumped up and down, clapping her hands in joy when she saw the new puppy.

An effective way for making showing writing come to life is to use acting. I worked with Erin Cole's fourth-grade class on showing writing using a Guess My Place activity. I asked Mrs. Cole to leave the room, and then I asked a student in the class to pick a place we could imagine ourselves in.

"The mall!" suggested Regina.

"Good idea," I said, and then asked each student to think of something they could do in the mall. Several students pretended to be shopping, others walked around, looking for items to "purchase," others pretended to play video games, and a few pretended to be eating and drinking. I asked them to mime all of these activities so that Mrs. Cole would need to use her powers of observation to determine the location. When she came in, it wasn't long before she said, "You're at the mall!"

As students returned to their seats, I asked them to think of words they could write that would make pictures in their minds about what they were doing. I asked that no one just write, "I went to the mall" or "I played video games." I encouraged them to think of what writers do when they write to make pictures in our minds.

All students wrote one or more sentences within minutes. While some were more successful than others at using good word choice, all of them succeeded in making a picture in our minds as readers. Here are a few examples from the class:

- Paige wrote: We went to the food court and got cool and refreshing water. In one second I changed from the sun to Pluto.
- Jamia wrote: It was a hot day so I went to the store and bought a Cherry Coke, and it was so delectable I scarcely took my time to drink it.
- Gavino described the arcade: I went to the arcade to play Tekken 4. I was pressing the buttons as fast as a jaguar so I could make it to the final level. When we finished we strolled around and talked about Game 5, the Yankees vs. the Red Sox.
- Deshaun wrote: I was so hot I bought a creamy vanilla ice cream. I started to bite the ice cream. It felt like I was diving into a pool filled with ice.

Showing vs. telling: The cornerstone of strong writing

The idea that showing writing is strong writing appears in one form or another in every book I have read on the writing process for adults or children. Any well-written children's book is full of examples of showing writing, and when students are grounded in the idea of showing writing, they will not be shy about pointing it out when they hear it. Two years ago I was reading aloud Kate DiCamillo's poignant *Because of Winn-Dixie* and my fifth graders stopped me on virtually every page to comment on the writing. I finally asked them to listen to the story for itself, and that we would talk about the writing separately. One danger about using mentor texts is that students may think that the only reason to read is to become a better writer. It is important to read for the sake of reading as well—students can learn about how to read certain texts as writers while reading other texts as readers.

Introducing the idea of showing writing can be done in many ways, but I try to get students to write in a showing way without telling them that is what they are doing. I typically ask a student from the class to come up in front of the room and act out an emotion I whisper to them. Once the acting begins, I ask the class to give me language to describe what they see. I ask the acting student not to speak, and so the words come directly from the image.

In Mrs. Cole's fourth-grade class, many students wanted to tell me the emotion they were witnessing when Jamia was acting happy.

"She's excited!" one student yelled.

"She's really happy," said another.

"What is she doing?" I asked them.

Before long, they were creating word pictures to describe Jamia's actions, and I recorded their descriptions:

> Jamia is jumping around.
> She is dancing and turning around.
> She is laughing.
> She is moving like crazy.
> Her braids are jumping around and her
>   barrettes are clinking together.
> Her mouth is falling open and her legs can't stop moving.

I then asked the class what emotion Jamia was acting out.

"She was happy," came the response.

I wrote "Jamia is happy" on the board, and labeled it as telling writing, and the descriptive writing as showing writing. We talked about the difference between the two types of writing, and how much better the showing writing described the emotion.

The reason I like to start with student writing to introduce the concept of showing vs. telling is because it enables students to think of themselves as writers. Highlighting student text as an example of what writers do helps to demystify the writing process. Students begin to see themselves as writers immediately. I believe many of even our youngest students have a sense of what good writing is all about, but if we do not point it out and identify it, they cannot concretely make the connection between what they do and what writers do.

Based on the samples listed above from Erin Cole's class, here is the list we came up with for what we noticed about showing writing:

- Good word choice / juicy words
- Specific nouns (I refer to these as "naming" words—for example, in the excerpts from the place activity above, specific brands of soda and video games are mentioned)
- Similes—(but, not too many!)
- Strong verbs
- Feeling words

After each of these were identified, I asked students to tell me exactly what they noticed in the student writing that caused them to share what they did. This creates the standard for always returning to the text when reading like a writer, whether the text is written by a student or by a published author.

Keep a word bank developed by students

In order to help students create pieces with stronger word choice, I encourage students to be word collectors. When we hear words we like in student writing, we write the words down. When we see or hear them in texts, we write them down. These words can become part of a word wall of describing words and verbs, or, they can just be alphabetized and updated for students to keep in their writing notebooks. I don't think it is necessary to use a thesaurus to have these words become part of a working vocabulary. In fact, as mentioned above, the thesaurus can lead to inauthentic writing. These lists of favorite words can be classroom-based, or they can be individual. Writers love words, and asking students to be on the hunt for words they love is yet another way to demystify the writing process.

Sometimes just changing the writing task to involve visualization helps students to create stronger images. I have used film clips to build word banks, and the visual media of film seems to help students come up with words they may not otherwise share.

Finding Nemo is full of action sequences. In Erin Cole's class, we watched a section of the film with sea turtles leading the main characters through a dangerous part of the ocean. We watched the film and then created this word bank of strong verbs to give language to what we just saw. I asked students what the fish and the turtles were *doing*, and this is the list of verbs they produced:

- squirming
- wobbling
- swimming
- flapping
- speeding
- shaking
- spinning

These strong verbs came from the visual image of film, and it can become part of a strong word bank. I have used the Michael Jordan film *To the Max* for this same purpose, and students developed lists of strong verbs from this film as well.

Highlight verbs, de-emphasize adjectives

When I ask students to help me make a sentence better, they often give me a string of adjectives because they believe that more is better. I asked a fourth-grade class to help me make this sentence better:

The leaves on the tree were pretty.

One student suggested:

The colorful, pretty, red and yellow leaves were pretty.

Admittedly, this is better, but the strings of adjectives don't make the writing sing. I think one key to helping the writing become stronger is to emphasize verbs rather than adjectives.

Given a sentence like the one above, I typically will praise a student for helping me, and admit that the writing is stronger. I then ask a follow-up question:

What are the leaves doing?

Sometimes I get some blank stares, but normally it isn't long before someone will attach a verb to the leaves. The point here is to make the leaves the subject, but to use a stronger, active verb rather than the passive "were." In the same class mentioned above, a student said:

The leaves were blowing in the wind and falling on the ground.

In another class, another student added:

Falling on the ground like rain!

Listening to our students, and encouraging this verbal word play, can give us so much as teachers. Sometimes we can use an anchor text from within our very own classrooms. The students in this class know about strong verbs, and they also know about similes. By simply asking them to think about what the objects they observe are doing, we can lift the level of the writing because of the use of interesting verbs.

Similes and other figurative language: What is appropriate for young writers?

Young writers use similes before they really know what they are. They notice them in books. One of my favorite lines in Jane Yolen's *Owl Moon* is on the very first page:

The trees stood still as giant statues. (Yolen 1987, p. 1)

Many older students know to call this a simile, but even the youngest writers I have worked with know that Yolen is comparing the trees to statues, and this is because the trees are very still. Once they notice it in text, they can then use it themselves. Some students call it "comparing writing," and if they do, I use their term alongside the word "simile" so that their thoughts are validated while I am teaching them a new term.

Similes are powerful tools, and they need to be used wisely and only where appropriate. Sometimes they are overused, and the power of the simile is lost. One way to help students use similes more judiciously is to spot how they are used in books you read aloud. Once they notice that they are not used in every paragraph, or even on every page, they can begin to understand how often to use them in their own pieces.

Simile hunt

Writing tends to be a sedentary activity, so moving to a new location can be a motivator for students. If the weather allows, I have taken students on a hunt for similes. I encourage them to yell out a simile when they see one. We take our writer's notebooks outside to record our thoughts, and when a student thinks of something to say, they share immediately:

> "The clouds look as soft as cotton!"
> "The swing set chain sounds like ice clinking in a glass!"
> "The grass looks like a huge green bed for taking a
> nap in!"

I typically stay outside for only five minutes, and then we spend another few minutes inside recording ideas and sharing our favorite similes. My goal in using this as an anchor writing activity is to make writing positive for students, and to encourage them to believe that they can produce good writing in a short amount of time.

If the weather does not allow for going outside, I have used the simile hunt in the building as well. This encourages students to see their school in new ways, as they search for interesting language to describe the everyday. When students ask me periodically if we can go on a simile hunt, I know I have succeeded in creating an anchor writing experience.

Using poetry year-round to lift the level of writing

Poetry is one of the best genres to use when asking students to lift the level of their writing. As Georgia Heard notes in her book *Awakening the Heart*, poetry is image-based, and the use of poetry can help our students become even more adept at focusing on making pictures in the reader's mind.

Poetry lessons that focus on observation and imagery help students become better writers. A unit of poetry that focuses only on form might cause students to identify poetry with only haiku and cinquains, poems that rely on syllabic patterns rather than on the images words can create. While these forms of poetry have their place, I have had success in helping students lift the level of their own writing when the focus of the poetry lessons is on words.

One of my favorite poetry assignments is the Six Room Poem described in *Awakening the Heart*. In this exercise, students write about a very specific place that is special to them using six different, very strong images. The first image they focus on is a description of what they see. The second is the quality of light. In the third room of the poem, they focus on sounds; in the fourth, what they wonder about; in the fifth, what they feel about the place; and in the sixth room they repeat their favorite phrases or words that they have already written.

When I introduce this activity to students, I ask them to bring in a photo of their favorite outdoor place. If they do not have a photo, I ask them to imagine it in their minds. I always have a few calendar pictures of beautiful outdoor places I bring with me for students who have trouble visualizing, or for students who may struggle with language. Looking at a picture helps students through the activity. I also use one of the calendar pictures as a model for my own writing.

I think the Six Room Poem works well as an anchor writing experience for students to develop image-based vocabulary because it requires students to write in multiple ways about one particular place. The writing is concrete because it is about one place, and time is allowed for students to really slow down and use their imaginations to help them use words to create pictures. Here is an example of a Six Room Poem from a fifth-grade student, Katherine:

Cocoa Beach

The palm trees swaying
Soothe my mind
Crashing waves
Tickle the bottoms of my feet
The sand is sandpaper rubbing at my feet
It soothes my sore feet
For they have been walking the
Endless sidewalk
Of concrete
But now the sound of the beach is
Deafening
Soothing
Homecoming
Now the glittering sun sets over the
Horizon
Now all there is to look at is the
Cotton candy clouds
I run into the ocean in my clothes
Splishing and
Splashing trying to keep my body warm
Besides the sounds of the ocean
Why is it so quiet?
Why is it so cold?
Why does it seem misty but it is clear?
These are the questions that will never be
Answered
But these are the things I wonder
As I float away on the
Ocean waves
As a Queen
Queen of the ocean.

Katherine was able to create this poem because she considered many images before she began composing. I have used the Six Room Poem idea in many classrooms in grades 3 through 6, and I am always impressed with the writing students produce from this exercise. Because it relies on a particular place, and a picture of a place can be used to help make the experience more concrete, I have used it effectively with many ELL students.

Here are a few examples of Six Room Poem ideas created by Linda Keoll's fourth-grade students:

Gentle Sounds

As the rain drops
on the rocks,
they pop like
popcorn.
I feel like I'm floating on a cloud
as I sit in the middle
of the delta I hear
voices of the
ocean calling me
triangular shapes
take me to the
voices of the ocean.
   —Aubrey

Quiet Place

As I lay there
On the grass
I saw the sun
Shining through the
Fluffy cotton ball clouds
Floating through the air.
 Shhhh . . .
 Shhhh . . .
 quiet
Listen to the
 wind
Whistling in the
Wild Daylight
 Sky.
 Shhhh . . .
 Shhhh . . .
 quiet
  Whooo!
   —Dalal

Great Mountains

As I lay there on the pointy
   green grass
I saw the white fluffy clouds
snow white cotton balls and
   huge mountains
Green leafy trees
   shadows from the trees
Sun shining
   through the clouds
Wind whistling
   in my ear
Silent breezes . . .
   peaceful
   Shhhh . . .
   Shhhh . . .
I wonder how tall
the mountains
are???
I wonder if there
is anyone else
besides my dad
and me??? I feel
relaxed. I am happy
I am really loved.
The wind whistling in
my ear.
      —Colton

Another poetry idea that encourages students to slow down and observe asks students to draw objects from nature. Valerie Worth's *All the Small Poems* is an excellent resource for well-crafted poems about ordinary objects. I use her poem "potatoes" to introduce the idea that we can find poetry everywhere. As I pass potatoes around the room, I encourage students to study the potato, and to listen to Valerie Worth's wise words about this seemingly common object. Because of the poem, students think very differently about words like "gnarl," "knob," and "dimple."

When using mentor text such as Worth's poem, I ask students to tell me what they notice. In Tamara Anglin's third-grade class, students came up with this list:

- The words don't rhyme
- Poems aren't like sentences
- It is written up and down instead of across
- It sounds good
- It is descriptive
- The words are not everyday words

We discuss how long the poet must have looked at the potato in order to write such a strong poem.

I have ready several types of flowers and foliage from a florist, in addition to shells and various types of squash. I model for them first what I would like them to do: draw their chosen object very large, and then label what they notice about the object after they draw it. I ask them to help me label various parts of my drawing by thinking of descriptive "not everyday" words. After the modeling, the students are ready to work, anxious to look and notice carefully.

The writing produced from such careful observation can help students to build their confidence. It can also help them to sustain their writing time for longer periods. The practice of writing poetry, because it is focused and helps students to write carefully, one word at a time, can inform all student writing.

ELL learners

All of the ideas listed in the chapter have been tried multiple times in various classrooms. Many of the classrooms I visit have a high percentage of ELL students and students who struggle with writing and students who are new to the writing process.

I have found when planning lessons that keeping in mind a few key points helps more students to be successful. I mention the use of acting in several of my lessons. This is not a gimmick—I use it because it is kinesthetic, and it makes words come to life. This helps ELL students, but it helps all students to make stronger pictures in their minds when we are discussing how to make our writing more interesting. As words are given to the actions, I write the words on chart paper, and this becomes part of the word bank accessible to ELL students. I often include visual cues for these words as well, adding symbols next to words so that ELL students can recall the words more easily.

I model everything I ask students to do in the writing workshop. Even in the drawing lesson mentioned above, I draw the object large on a piece of chart paper, and I ask students to tell me what they notice. I make sure that they can see that I want them to fill their pages with their drawings, because this will help them to notice things they normally would pass over. When I write, I often model what I *don't* want them to do, and see if they notice. For example, after a student acts out an emotion as part of practicing showing writing, I might write on the board "She was sad," and wait for students to tell me that I could use better words.

I worked with Debbie Smith's third-grade class on writing small poems about food, which is described above. The majority of Debbie's third graders are ELL students, from far corners of the Earth: Africa, Asia, Latin America, and Mexico are only some of the places Debbie's students have come from. I always model more specifically when working with ELL students, so on the day I visited her class to talk about writing small poems, I brought in three food items: limes, kiwi, and fresh ginger root. I chose these foods because they can be used to develop distinct sensory images. We all read the poem "potatoes" in Valerie Worth's book *All the Small Poems* from a piece of chart paper, and then we developed a word bank for each of our food items.

For limes, the class created this list:

> Green and yellow
> Soft and smooth
> Bumpy like Braille
> Looks like a full moon
> Looks like a tennis ball

We developed similar lists for kiwi fruit and ginger, as these food items were passed around our group gathered on the floor.

Then, prior to students selecting their food item for writing a poem, we wrote a group poem for limes:

Limes
They are green as grass
And yellow like sunspots
They are smooth
And soft as a baby's cheeks
And look like
A full moon
They are very juicy
I like limes
But do you?

Because of the word bank, the model poem, and the ability to examine the food itself, all students were able to craft their own poem, even those who had recently arrived in this country.

I believe we must aim high to keep all students engaged. If we expect our students to be strong writers, they are more likely to produce strong writing. We must scaffold these experiences for our struggling writers, and we must help our ELL writers with clear, visual models and word banks, but we all must write, and write well. When I learn that a class I am going to work with has five ELL students, eight students who receive extra help because of academic struggles, and four who hate to write, I can easily become overwhelmed and decide to create a low-level, simple writing assignment. Or, I can ask students to notice how amazing the written word is, get them excited about creating pictures in readers' minds, develop a love of language that makes them want to write, to tell stories, to create poems. I always err on the side of assuming all students can produce strong writing when given the proper support.

Final thoughts

Focusing on word choice helps students believe that writing is manageable. Sentences, poems, stories, and entire novels are all written the same way: one word at a time. Children are fascinated by words, and love to play with different word meanings from the time they are young. When we capitalize on this fascination, we can encourage even our most reluctant writers to begin thinking of writing as something enjoyable, something possible. We reap what we sow as writing teachers: if we focus only on correctness, it is hard to imagine a group of students who will rise to the challenge of wanting to write in beautiful, image-based prose. But if we can help our students love words, we will witness students who cannot wait to put their thoughts on the page.

{ CHAPTER 4 }

How Can I Help Students Write in Complete and More Interesting Sentences?

When our students write in their journals, craft stories, and develop ideas in research reports, they struggle at times with how best to craft their ideas into written words. One of the first questions my students ask is, "Does it have to be in complete sentences?" If students have had time to orally rehearse what they are going to write about, and they have a plan or a draft of their writing, I do ask them to write in complete sentences. Many of my most reluctant or struggling writers over the years do not have a sense of sentence structure, and repetitive worksheets asking them to identify fragments and run-ons do not generally impact their own writing. They still do not recognize when they are writing in incomplete sentences, or when they are stringing along many ideas with a series of *ands*. As I walk around a classroom and look at student work, one of the first things I notice is if students have a sense of sentence structure. Some students, even in fifth grade, eliminate all capitals and punctuation while they write. How can I help them to understand the idea of a sentence?

Look at student writing carefully to determine sentence structure needs

I have tried many techniques over the years to help students who struggle with sentences. It took me a long time to move away from thinking that virtually no one in my class knew how to write a sentence to understanding that I needed to find the nature and scope of the problem. The first thing I do now is figure out exactly which students need extra support. I can find this out by simply reminding students, calmly and without interrupting their thoughts, to write in sentences, or to remember capitals and periods in their writing. Often, as Lucy Calkins so wisely suggests in her *Units of Study for Primary Writing* series, if we just praise one or two students for remembering to use capitals and periods, much of the rest of the class will follow suit. The problem I have found with waiting until the writing proceeds halfway down a page with no sentence breaks is that the student then has to go back and try to find and fix errors in a sea of text. If I gently remind students about sentences *as* they are writing, however, I can determine who struggles, and who may just need a reminder.

If I collect student writing and notice many students have made sentence errors, I often will give the writing back, uncorrected, with a colored pen (not red), and ask students to spend a few minutes to see if they can correctly mark their capitals and ending punctuation. Doing this allows me to discover more about my class: I will now know who can identify their sentences with just a reminder, versus students who can find some of the sentences, versus students who cannot determine where sentence breaks belong. I now have instructional groupings. The more I keep with student work, rather than pre-packaged sentence worksheets, the more luck I have had in getting students to write in complete sentences in their own writing. For students who really struggle, and still cannot write in complete sentences, I often ask them to pause in their writing when they think they have a sentence, and to see me before they continue on to their next sentence. Over time, this technique has been helpful for students who do not at first grasp the idea of structuring writing in complete sentences.

The process of helping students identify sentences in their writing is ongoing, but it only answers the question about helping students produce complete sentences. What about sentence writing as a craft? What are some ways to help students go beyond common sentence beginnings and to think about how they might craft some stronger writing?

Teach students to notice sentence structures in their own writing and in professional writing to craft stronger pieces

Students often write about themselves in school: they write about their experiences, their favorite sports and foods, their families, their hopes and dreams. A common concern can surface in this type of writing: students often begin many of their sentences with *I.* The way to determine if this is a problem is to examine student work, and if the problem appears, I write my own paragraph with this same type of problem. Below is an example of a paragraph I wrote when working with a group of fourth and fifth graders in Judy Patterson and Karen Ackerman's class who were struggling with beginning most of their sentences with *I:*

I like to eat pizza. I could even eat it every day. I like pepperoni pizza, sausage pizza, and mushroom pizza. I would eat anything, as long as it is on a pizza! I ask for extra cheese. I like to stretch the cheese out from my mouth. I always save the crust for last. I like the taste of the chewy crust as I finish my pizza. I like pizza because it makes me happy!

I asked the students what they noticed about the writing, to see first if they would pick up on the sentence beginnings. Comments ranged from: "It is all on topic" to "You really like pizza!" I asked them to circle the first word in each sentence, and then a student immediately said, "You started each sentence with I!" I asked them if they noticed they often did the same thing in their writing, and they concurred that they did.

Working together as a group, we discussed how to solve the problem. This is what they came up with:

I like to eat pizza every day. Pepperoni, mushroom, and sausage are my favorite toppings. If it is on a pizza, I will eat it! I ask for extra cheese so I can stretch it from my mouth. The chewy crust is my favorite part, so I save it for last. Pizza makes me happy!

I was pleased that students found ways to develop a new paragraph, this time without the repetitive sentence beginnings. It is important to mention to students during this work that it is necessary to begin some sentences with *I*—the key is to not overdo it. One way to solve this problem is to ask students to read their work aloud. In similar exercises I have done with classes, by the time I read the third or fourth sentence aloud in a paragraph written like the one above, students stop me and tell me I began every sentence with *I*. Students can notice the same things if they read their own work aloud.

After we completed the group paragraph about pizza, paying attention to the sentence structure and word choice, I asked students to write their own pieces about their favorite foods. I gave them a few minutes to talk with partners, and then we wrote for about fifteen minutes. Here are some sample sentences from their work:

Eating cherries reminds me of the center of a red firework. Personally, I like my cherries without pits, but if my cherries had them, I wouldn't mind. As I pull the stem from my mouth I feel sad that I have no more cherries to eat. I love cherries anywhere, anytime at all. (Katie)

I love to eat ice cream every day. When I eat it, it reminds me of a cold winter day when there is a blizzard. If you like ice cream as much as I do, you would eat it every day for dessert. (Vicky)

Sentence beginnings are not the only issue with student writing. Often, especially while writing research reports, students develop pieces composed of overly short and simple sentences.

Use professional writing to craft stronger sentences

I worked with a group of Rhonda Prendergast's second graders while they were researching penguins. When I asked them what they knew, students raised their hands, eager to share. I was amazed at their level of knowledge:

> "Penguins have a tooth they use when they are babies to get out of their eggs."
>
> "Father penguins keep their eggs warm on their feet!"
>
> "Mother penguins go out to sea for a few days to get food, and when they get back, they regurgitate the food into their babies' mouths."
>
> "Penguins huddle together to keep warm."
>
> "They molt in the spring."

Obviously, this class knew their penguins! Even though the class ranged greatly in their reading level, their teacher, Rhonda, masterfully helped all students to gain in their knowledge of these most interesting birds. Students had ample access to reading material on their level, they had been taught reading strategies to help them with informational text, they had seen films, explored the Internet, and had many class discussions about their learning.

Now it was time to write. Their teacher was frustrated, because so often students resort to simple sentences, just relaying the facts, or they copy directly from other text when they are writing factual research reports. Clearly, the students knew a lot of amazing things about penguins, but could they write in more interesting ways about these animals they had come to love?

When I want to help students develop their own craft as writers, I try to find a professional example of the type of writing they are trying to produce. One of my favorite texts about animals is *Gentle Giant Octopus* by Karen Wallace. In this book, Wallace tells the story of one mother octopus trying to find a den where she can lay her eggs. Embedded in each

Using strong writing as a model

page of this beautifully illustrated book are the facts about the octopus she used to tell this one tale. The text toggles back and forth from facts to story, all of it carefully researched and scientifically accurate. Because I do not want students to focus in on the octopus, I tell them the purpose for my sharing sections of the book. I model through the use of a think-aloud, as described in *Strategies That Work* by Harvey and Goudvis. Students benefit greatly from hearing teachers clearly explain their thinking.

> "I am going to share only parts of this book with you today because we are going to talk about writing good sentences. You know so much about penguins, and now it is time to write, so we need to think about what writers do. I am going to first tell you something that Karen Wallace, the author of the book, learned about the giant octopus while she did her research."

On a piece of chart paper, I have written the following sentences in blue marker:

> A giant octopus is very big. The giant octopus has tentacles.

Then I open to a page in the book where Karen Wallace has written:

> The giant octopus is huge, like a giant spaceship. Long tentacles fly like ribbons behind her.

I have already written these sentences in red marker underneath the facts recorded in blue. I look at the students:

"I wonder why Karen Wallace decided to write her ideas this way [I point to the words in red] instead of just copying down the facts? What is different about the words in red, the words Karen Wallace chose, and the words in blue?"

Hands go up:

"The red writing is more exciting," one student shares.

"It has more details," says another.

I try to push the students a little bit further.

"Which part is more exciting?" I ask. "Come up and circle the words you think are more exciting."

One student comes up and circles the word *spaceship*. I then ask: "Why is this more exciting?"

"Because it makes it more interesting."

"So, when we write, is one of our jobs to make it more interesting?" I ask these types of questions because I want students to think like writers. They are in charge of the writing they produce, and I want them to see themselves as writers who make the same kinds of choices that authors make.

During this conversation, I am pointing to the picture in the book, reminding students that Karen Wallace came up with her ideas because she looked at pictures of an octopus. I invite the students to "think like Karen":

"Can anyone think like Karen for a minute, look at this picture of the octopus, and think about what else she could have written? She wrote that the octopus looks like a giant spaceship. What else could she have written? What else does it look like?"

In just a few moments, these are the types of responses I receive:

> A big thumb
> A balloon with spider legs attached
> A big spider underwater

Students are definitely thinking like writers now. I review with them what they have said about writing. I write on the chart paper near the red writing:

> More exciting
> Details

I ask them: "Is there anything else you notice about the writing?"

"It has expression," Noah says.

"What do you mean?" I ask him.

"It expresses something different. It isn't just facts," Noah responds.

"So, when we write, is it our job to not just write facts, but to think of something different or new? Can we do that today?"

I add to our list: Expresses a new idea.

I want to connect these thoughts quickly to ideas about penguins, so I tell them something I know about a penguin that their teacher has given me information about. I write on the chart paper and say aloud:

> "The Fiordland penguin has a yellow crest on the top of his head.
>
> I am writing this in blue on the chart paper because it is a fact. I am wondering if we can do the work Karen Wallace did and write it in a more interesting way. I wonder if we can think of something new to say, like Noah suggested. Close your eyes. Picture a penguin with a yellow crest around his head. Can we do better than just writing the facts?"

I have shown them a picture of the penguin so that they can make a picture in their minds. Then, I wait a few minutes while they close their eyes, trying to think of what they could say instead of just the facts. Here are some of the ideas they mention:

> It is the color of the sun
> It looks like a headband
> It looks like a circle around his head

"These are great ideas!" I tell them. "You are doing exactly what writers do: they try to think of new ways to write information!"

Combining some of the students' suggestions, I write on the chart paper, in red, underneath the blue penguin fact:

> The Fiordland penguin has a sun-colored crest that looks like a yellow headband.

I go back to the list of qualities they noticed about Karen Wallace's writing to check to see if I have accomplished my goals:

"Did I make it more exciting? Did I add details? Did I think of something new?"

The students agree that I accomplished these goals, so I asked them to think of something they might write about what their penguin looked like. Could they write something new from the facts, something exciting that added details to their writing? Below are some of the things these second-grade students wrote during writer's workshop that day:

> Cashion worked with a simile and a strong verb in these sentences: Penguins have stomachs as white as snow. They toboggan like a sled on a cold winter night.
>
> Josiah was thinking of football players when he wrote this simile: Penguins huddle like football players on Saturday night at the great game.
>
> Jenacie filled her page with descriptive writing: The king penguin toboggans to sea to get delicious plankton, krill, and fish, and squid. When the mom penguin is at sea the egg hatches a cute puffy fuzzy baby penguin out. The dad penguin gives the baby milk.
>
> Arianna compared her penguin to another animal: The little blue penguin waddles like a duck on a sunny day.

Modeling for ELL students

In the class mentioned above, there were a few ELL students, but I have also worked in a similar fashion with teachers who had a large number of ELL students. The modeling was more structured, and visual cues were key throughout the lesson. In Debbie Smith's third-grade class, students were researching animals from Australia, rather than one common animal. As in the class discussed above, Debbie had provided students with a mix of visual materials and reading materials. Students had seen films, read and looked at books, and shared a lot of information about their animals with the class. When it came time to write, Debbie shared Rhonda's goal: she wanted to make sure students didn't just copy sentences from the book.

We structured the learning carefully by beginning with a brain-stormed list of action words students could use in their writing. The action words helped because they were easy to visualize, and because we could act them out. When we mentioned that a dingo could sneak up on a lizard, for example, we had a picture of a dingo, a picture of a lizard, and we then asked the students to pretend to be a dingo catching a lizard by sneaking up on him. They enjoyed acting this out. I wrote on chart paper: "The dingo sneaks up on the lizard" instead of "The dingo catches the lizard."

We followed this same procedure for eating. "How would a dingo eat a lizard?" we asked. Students held an imaginary lizard in their hands, and pretended to eat it. Would a dingo nibble a lizard? What would that look like? Would it gobble a lizard? How is that different? This procedure was followed for many animals. Below are some examples of the type of writing that resulted.

Tom wrote about the koala bear:

> The koala nibbles the eucalyptus tree leaves. They try to find juicy fruit and grab and nibble it. Sometimes they go down and lick the ground.

Tom also used similes on another page of his book to describe his researched animal:

> The fat koala has claws as sharp as a knife. The cute koala has legs as short as a head. The fuzzy koala has fur as gray as a rock. The soft koala has eyes as wide as paper.

Mahmoud wrote about the echidna:

> The black echidna has a tongue as slippery as soap. The slow echidna has thorns as sharp as a knife. The tiny echidna has a pouch as small as an anthole. The long echidna has a hand as tiny as a shoe.

Finally, Diana had this to tell us about the wallaby:

The wallaby can nibble plants and grass. The wallaby swallows the plants and gets water from the plants. The wallaby will not nibble food. It will just swallow it.

Debbie Smith, through her careful modeling, encouragement, and use of visuals, has helped her ELL students to succeed at a very high level. She is a teacher who has proven that high expectations result in quality writing.

Final thoughts

Through the experiences mentioned above, and through dialogues with many teachers in different grade levels, I am convinced that the way to help students craft better sentences is no different from the way we help them to become better writers: we ask them to write. When we ask students to produce writing, we can get physical evidence of their understanding of sentence structures. When we talk to them about what we notice as they are writing, or provide models of well-written sentences in a story or nonfiction text, then we can begin to help them become more adept at using their sentence knowledge in effective ways. Students should not be limited to writing one sentence in primary grades because they have a difficult time deciding where the punctuation will go. In fact, I would argue the opposite: students should be encouraged to write stories, letters, and factual reports so that they see a reason to write multiple sentences. Once there are enough words on the page, the discussion about sentences can begin. Students will become better at writing in a variety of sentence structures as they get more comfortable with the act of writing.

{CHAPTER 5}

How Can I Help My Students Organize Their Writing?

A few years ago, I was working with my students on narrative writing. I pulled out a planning guide prior to writing our stories, and it advised story writers to think of the characters, setting, problem, rising action, and resolution prior to writing a story. As a class, we looked at some of our favorite picture books, identifying the various recommended elements of plot structure. Then, I asked my students to organize their own stories using this planner. I thought all was going well until I picked up the drafts of the stories. Almost everyone had identifiable elements of a story, but the flow was missing. The writing seemed stilted because students were paying so much attention to the plan they created that they didn't engage the reader in a story. Some students spent two pages describing characters, and others created a hybrid between a story and the plan for a story. Since that time, I have thought a lot about what may have gone wrong, and I think I have approached a possible answer: I asked students to organize their thinking in a way that was not conducive to the final result. I looked again at some of my favorite stories to try and figure out what went wrong.

In *Owl Moon*, we do not know the exact age of the girl, we do not know the color of her father's hair, nor his height. The setting is made very clear throughout the narrative, but we do not know what town or state the action takes place. What we do know is that, on the very first page in the very first sentence, something *happens*—a girl and her father go out one winter night, hoping to see an owl:

> Late one winter night, long past my bedtime, Pa and I went owling. (Yolen 1987, p. 1)

The age of the girl is inferred (it is long past her bedtime, so she must be young), and we know she is with her father. More important, and more exciting for the reader, is the promise of action: they are going out one night to *do something*. We like stories when something happens, and yet many story organizers suggest students focus on descriptions of characters and settings first, and this results in stories that begin with more description than action.

Another picture book with a strong narrative hook is Faith Ringgold's beautiful *Tar Beach*. Cassie, the narrator of the tale, describes the night the stars lift her up and she flies over Harlem, watching her friends and family down below:

> I will always remember when the stars fell down around me and lifted me up above the George Washington Bridge. I could see our tiny rooftop, with Mommy and Daddy and Mr. and Mrs. Honey, our next-door neighbors, still playing cards as if nothing was going on, and Be Be, my baby brother, lying real still on the mattress, just like I told him to, his eyes like huge floodlights tracing me through the sky. (Ringgold 1991, pp. 1, 2)

Like Yolen, Ringgold has a strong beginning because something happens, and this creates a narrative that readers want to hear. The organizer I had provided for my students did not result in the type of writing I was hoping for, and my students were disappointed in their own efforts.

Since that time, I have taken a hard look at asking students to plan, or "pre-organize" their writing. I learned that for some students, the plan itself was a detriment because it took them so long to plan for their writing that they weren't spending enough time writing. Other students might be so connected to their organizational plan that they do not stray from it while they write. This creates writing that shows no evidence of the process of writing, which includes learning where the writing might take you. This is not to say that some students are not helped by using some type of organizer; there are times when a plan can help to keep the writing focused and clear. The organizational needs of students vary widely, depending on the purpose for writing, and on the group of students. When thinking about helping students with organization, then, it is important to consider the genre and then the specific needs of the students.

Provide students with various methods for organizing writing

One organizing tool cannot be used for all the types of writing we ask students to produce. In the following section, I will discuss some of the tools I have used effectively with students, but this is not meant to be an exhaustive list. The best way to measure the success of an organizing tool or a planner is to look at the writing. Our students can also provide insights into the effectiveness of these tools during class discussions.

Visual tools

Graphic organizers are common in helping students plan for stories. One of the planners many students use is a web: a diagram with a large circle in the middle surrounded by a series of smaller circles. Many students I work with are comfortable with webs, and I have used them successfully with certain types of writing. During brainstorming sessions, for example, I might ask students to use the center circle of a topic, and then to use the circles around the web for details. I might also use the web if I want students to think about everything they know about something; rather than list everything, they can use the web format to visualize how everything they know (the details) connects to the main idea (the circle in the middle).

Webs can cause problems for some students once the writing begins, however. For example, a student may create a web with the word dog in the middle. Then, details in surrounding circles may contain names of dog breeds. If the web stops here, a student could likely produce a stilted piece of writing that merely lists facts:

> There are many breeds of dogs. There are poo-
> dles, dachshunds, chows, and beagles. There are
> many types of dogs.

Even if a supporting detail is given for each of the breeds, the web planner can lead to just a list of facts if the student has little to say about a topic.

In Mrs. McMullen's fourth-grade classroom, listing was a problem, and so we wanted to know if the students were creating lists because their planning was ineffective. I created my own web, with list-like writing resulting from it, to see if the students would notice how the web had steered me in the wrong direction.

The students were studying explorers who came to Colorado, so my web had the topic "Colorado Explorers" in the center. I then used several circles, equally spaced around the center circle to complete the web. In these circles, I included brief phrases: hard to farm, many died, gold rush, weather in mountains, dust storms. I produced this paragraph from the web:

Coming to Colorado

When settlers came to Colorado in the 1800s, they had to work hard. The eastern plains were dry and it was hard to farm. Some settlers hoped to find gold. When they traveled they had to come by wagon. Dust storms were a problem. Many people died before they got to Colorado. The mountains were high, and sudden changes in weather even in the summer made it hard to travel. Some towns grew quickly because gold was found, and then everyone thought they would find gold too.

I asked students what they noticed about the writing.

John noticed that the two sentences about the gold rush were separated in the paragraph. He suggested that they be placed together so that the ideas would be more clear.

Zhane mentioned that the paragraph did not focus on one idea, but many. She suggested I just focus the paragraph on one idea, and add more details.

Many students said that the paragraph did not answer questions like why, how, or when things happened. Like Zhane, they suggested that I add more specific details to the paragraph.

This discussion set the stage for thinking about different ways to plan for writing. I asked students to think about ways we could plan our writing that would help us, rather than cause us to write in lists. We talked about the importance of a main idea, and then supporting details, but the problem with a web is that these details might really be big ideas. If they are, then the writing becomes a list, as shown above.

Graphic organizers that more closely connect to the purpose of the writing are more useful than just always relying on a web. For example, if the purpose of the writing is to give many details about dog breeds, then students should plan accordingly. A graphic organizer that may assist students can look like a web, with more branches for details about each breed. Once the web is filled in with details, it can be examined and sorted to determine which details to include, and which ones to possibly eliminate.

If the purpose of the writing is to tell about one particular breed, then some characteristics should be determined prior to creating the planner. The breed's name could appear in the middle of the web, for example, but then the characteristics of the breed can be listed in their own section, with room for several details. The point is to create a planner that makes sense: one that will provide students with a scaffold to list the kinds of interesting details that will result in a well-written product. Webs can be helpful, but to avoid list-like writing with few details, it is important to look at the word in the center of the web. Broad topics lead to lists, as shown in the Colorado piece above. Narrowing the focus of the topic in the middle to something specific such as "Gold Rush in Colorado" or "Miners in Colorado" may help students to organize their writing because as they add details to their webs, they can check to see if they have enough information to even create a piece of writing.

But not all students need a web, even when creating expository text. I often ask students to come up with their own suggestions for creating planning tools.

In two third-grade classrooms, students were getting ready for writing to the prompt "Describe something you like to do in your free time." Prior to writing, I asked the students to plan their writing and gave them three minutes to plan. I encouraged them to do whatever made sense to them: they could draw a picture, write some words, make a web, or plan in any way they thought would be helpful. After three minutes, several students shared their planners, which varied widely.

Student-generated planners

Michelle developed a web with the word *Disneyland* in the middle and details in spokes around the center circle. She used specific details in her web (fake crystal glow in the cave, favorite ride, fast as a cheetah, scary, dark caves), and these details helped her in her writing. She focused her ideas around one ride even though her center circle was the broader topic of Disneyland.

Lea created a series of triangles with words and pictures inside them. She labeled the triangles "freeze tag," "playhouse," "bowling," and "golf." She marked an "x" by freeze tag and explained to the class that the "x" meant she wanted to write about freeze tag. Lea did something totally different from Michelle: she thought about many different things she could possibly write about, and then chose her favorite topic from these choices. Her writing was focused completely on freeze tag, and like Michelle, she avoided creating a mere list. She slowed down and added specific details.

Alyssa created two webs: one for scooters, and one for Disney World. When she explained the webs to the class, she said, "I changed to Disney World because I didn't have enough to say about scooters." I praised Alyssa for her self-awareness: she knew from her plan that she needed to change her mind, so she created an effective plan for her purposes. Alyssa chose to write about Disney World because her initial planner helped her to see that she had more to say about this topic.

No one plan can work for every student, and we might learn a lot about what works best by asking our students to explain what works best for them.

I often ask students to talk through their ideas for writing with a partner. This verbal rehearsal can help students organize their thoughts prior to writing, and it can also verify that they have chosen a good topic.

Verbal rehearsal prior to writing

In a second-grade classroom, students were working on stories about their lives, but the teacher wanted to make sure that students would have enough to write about a topic before they began their writing. When students run out of ideas to write about on one topic, they often just begin writing about something else rather than trying to add details to their initial idea.

I modeled my own planning for the students by closing my eyes and talking about what I was going to write about. I told them I was making a picture in my head as I was planning my writing:

"I am thinking about telling the story about the time I was looking for my friend's cat, Milo. Milo was staying with me because my friend was on vacation. When I came home, I couldn't find him. I looked in the kitchen, and then under the couch, and then I finally heard him meowing in the bathroom."

I told the class that I knew I had a good story because I could make clear pictures in my mind about what happened. My verbal rehearsal was short, but I had more to say. I asked students to close their eyes and picture their story. After about thirty seconds, I asked them to turn to a partner. After determining who would speak first, students had thirty seconds to share their story with their partner. I challenged each of them:

"When I ask you to stop, you should have more to say! Don't just say: 'I went to the swimming pool' or 'I like to play with my dog.' Really think of the details so that you can tell your partner a story!"

After thirty seconds, I asked the students to stop, and then I immediately asked who had more to say. Many hands went up. I asked a few of these students to share their ideas out loud, so the rest of the class could hear how this student was planning. This type of planning is very efficient: in less than three minutes, I have modeled my ideas, students have shared in partners, and a few students have shared with the class. Verbal rehearsal can also be very effective because it can immediately identify the students who may need help with their writing, and they won't be sitting in front of a blank piece of paper waiting for you to notice. If I notice some students had nothing to share during the partnered verbal rehearsal, I meet with them while other students have begun their writing to help them pick an idea to write about.

Planning and organizing narrative fiction: Focusing on events

As I mentioned in the beginning of this chapter, my journey into examining the effectiveness of planners for writing began with narratives. After many false starts, I have found that focusing on events can help students to plan well-crafted narratives. If the purpose of the writing is to tell a story, the plan should focus on actions: a series of rectangles for students to sketch what happened in the beginning, a few boxes for the middle events, and then one box for the end. This type of planner resembles the mock-up for film stories or a comic strip. By focusing on the events of a story, the piece is organized around a narrative to begin with, rather than on a main idea and supporting details.

Since the narrative planner is primarily visual and focuses on actions, I like to use wordless picture books as narrative models. *Tuesday*, by David Weisner, serves this purpose, and it meets the needs of all students in the class: even ELL students can understand the narrative because it is not focused on words to tell a story. Weisner's tale begins in the swamp, where one Tuesday at nightfall frogs begin to float on their lily pads. Before long, they are flying through the town, getting stuck in sheets, flying through living rooms, being chased by a dog, and then chasing a dog. In the morning, the frogs unexpectedly fall and return to the swamp, leaving a pile of lily pads in their wake. The illustrations in the story always cause a reaction: students laugh at the detailed drawings, and love to anticipate what will happen next. I use this story to talk about the structure of narrative:

"What happens at the beginning of the story?"

"Frogs fly!"

"Exactly—and what happens next?"

The story works well because the narrative is contained: there is a clear beginning action, with several actions in the middle of the story before a surprise ending. The events in the middle make the narrative more interesting, but the story is not novel-length. I think students are often frustrated when they realize they cannot sustain writing long enough to create the books they love the most, such as the *Harry Potter* series. I have worked with many students who simply abandon their attempts at narrative because they can't create what they read. Sharing books like *Tuesday* makes writing narratives more approachable.

After we discuss the story of the flying frogs as a series of events, I often begin a narrative study with a picture to motivate a story. A very helpful tool for this is a series of posters by Chris Van Allsburg called *The Mysteries of Harris Burdick*. In these posters, the author of *Two Bad Ants* and *Jumanji* creates images that beg to become stories. One poster shows a man holding a chair over his head, ready to hit a lump under his rug. A lamp on the table just above the lump is about to fall. I use this picture and ask students to help me create a narrative, with the man about to hit the lump as the opening action.

In Jan Adair's fourth-grade class, we had examined *Tuesday* for narrative structure, and we were ready to begin our own narrative. Using the *Harris Burdick* poster of the man about to hit the lump under the rug, we decided to make the narrative come to life. I chose someone from the class to be the man holding the chair, and another student to be the lump by crouching down on the floor. We created a narrative together as a class, and counted on one hand the number of events we wanted to include: I encouraged students to think about the beginning of their story as the thumb of one hand, three main events in the middle of their story as the middle fingers, and the end of the story as the pinky. Students held up their fingers or their thumb as we created the story as a visual reminder of how close we were to the end of the tale. The physical reminder provided by telling the tale on our fingers helps the narrative to remain more controlled.

As we wrote the tale together, I told students that I was going to use many of the ideas the class suggested, and incorporate as many good thoughts as I could. I sketched each event in the story and then labeled the event with a few words. I used sketches as a visual cue to help all students visualize the tale, but to also help ELL students understand that we were recording the events of the tale being acted out by classmates. My goal was to work quickly so that students could get to their own writing as soon as possible.

The story Jan's class created was full of events, listed below as beginning, middle, and end details:

> Beginning: One night, Mr. Sawyer saw a big lump under the rug and he picked up a chair to hit it.
>
> Middle: The lamp fell off the table when the lump moved. Mr. Sawyer was about to hit the lump when he heard a meow. He was relieved, thinking the lump was just his pet cat hiding from him, so he dropped the chair. Suddenly, Mr. Sawyer realized the meow was coming from behind him. The lump was not his cat! The lump made a squeaking noise, and Mr. Sawyer lifted the rug up to see a mouse.
>
> End: Mr. Sawyer decided to keep the mouse as a pet, even though it made the cat mad.

As students thought about their own stories, I asked them to think about interesting events, and to sketch them quickly on paper as a kind of rehearsal prior to writing. Students were welcomed to verbally rehearse their own version of the story, and I encouraged them to use the fingers on their hand to recount key events. Since the class was involved in creating the group narrative, I allowed them to use any two events from the class story in their own version of the tale. This technique both honors the work the class has done, and allows all writers to succeed.

I have had great success in helping students write narratives when using this approach to planning and organization. When students focus on the events of the narrative, it is possible that characters or setting may not be clear, but this can be a point for revision. I want students to get to the writing as quickly as possible without being bogged down in a plan or in a narrative that goes nowhere. By quickly visualizing the events in a story, they can more effectively produce a narrative.

Here is a first draft of a story by Mariah, a student in Jan's class. She wrote this story after completing a plan with captioned pictures.

One cold, dark night, Tammy had just come home from work and decided to send a message to her friend on the computer. Then, she heard her dog growling at a little lump under her rug. The lump started to run away from the hissing dog. Tammy got up from her computer chair and walked up to the dog and put it in the back yard. Then, she went and slowly picked up the rug, and found a guinea pig under the rug!

Tammy picked up the tiny guinea pig, and it bit Tammy. Then, she dropped the guinea pig on the rug. She picked the guinea pig up and she put it in a box. Then, the guinea pig started to squeak in a frightened voice.

The next morning Tammy went and bought the guinea pig a cage, food, a bowl, and other things he needed. Tammy decided to keep the guinea pig as a pet. She named him Anthony. After Tammy got back from the store she put Anthony in his cage with fresh food and water. Anthony was happy, but the dog was very unhappy. The dog was just waiting for the day Tammy would leave the guinea pig's cage open. . .

Mariah demonstrates the ability to create a clear narrative organized in a series of events. Though the class model helped her, Mariah's story is unique and full of her own ideas.

Final thoughts

We must remember that writing is a process, so requiring an organizer prior to writing may actually get in the way of students producing strong writing. If they spend too much time organizing, they may not want to write. I have particularly noticed this in second- and third-grade classrooms.

If we want students to organize their writing effectively, we must first decide what we want students to produce. If they are to produce narrative fiction, then, as shown above, it might help students to visualize their narrative before writing. I have had students ask me if they must complete the visual planner prior to writing, and I have told them no. Sometimes, getting the ideas down in writing helps some students produce more writing, and the ideas flow as they write. They can change their minds as they go.

If we want students to produce a nonfiction piece about a topic they know a lot about, then they should see models of the types of writing they can produce, and then they can plan accordingly. As mentioned above, for some students a web may work, but for others a verbal rehearsal may be more effective, or just writing itself may help students to organize their thoughts.

Of all the methods described above, I have found the verbal rehearsal to be the most effective. I think it lends itself to all types of writing because if students can talk about what they are going to write, then they are more likely to feel confident about the writing itself.

{ CHAPTER 6 }

How Can I Help My Students Use Revision Effectively?

Revision is a key to strong writing. Students often are reluctant to revise for many reasons: they may honestly like what they have written in a first draft, they do not want to spend the time to go back and look at their own writing again, or they see writing as something that's finished once it is on the page.

I have tried many ways to help students see revision as important to writing, but the most successful method has been to incorporate it as part of the process. Waiting until writing is far along can result in students being less willing to change something. Once too many words are on the page, revising seems like a daunting task.

When I first started using the process approach to writing nearly twenty years ago, I asked students to revise every piece of writing they completed. This isn't what someone told me to do; I just saw it as my job. We would work for a week or two on a piece, and I would ask my sixth graders to read over their drafts, revise them, and then turn in a final copy with their draft. Typically, little would be changed from the draft to the final. I look back and realize that I was not teaching my students about revision as part of the process of writing, and I was confusing editing with revision.

Separate revision from editing for mechanics

In order to help students separate editing from revision, we must show them the difference. Modeling the practice of revision is a way to make the experience more concrete for students, and also to show them the rewards of revising. If they associate revision with something negative, or something they must go *back* and do, then it will be less appealing.

I think that one of the problems we bring as teachers of writing is our own baggage. As a teacher who truly loves to read, and who wants to instill a love of reading and literature in my students, I would never share negative experiences about reading. I would never introduce a book and say, "I hated reading this when I was your age, and now it is your turn!" This sounds extreme, but when I think about this type of scenario in the context of writing instruction, I do not know how extreme it is. How often do we share positive experiences about writing with our students? I remember many occasions when I told students about my strict English teachers in high school, long before computers, when I had to carefully type and retype draft after draft until it was perfect. I have told stories of my teacher from high school who taught me to love literature, but who would automatically drop an entire letter grade from a paper if it contained the words "a lot" as one word. Many of us, even those of us who love to teach writing, have ambiguous or even negative relationships with the revision process, so we must first convince ourselves, with our own writing, that revision need not be painful. The reverse, in fact, is true.

If I assign something for my students to write, I begin by writing it myself. Two years ago, I worked on my own research alongside my fifth graders while they uncovered details about unsolved mysteries such as the Loch Ness monster, UFOs, and Stonehenge. I studied the *Mary*

Begin with your own writing

Celeste, a ship whose crew mysteriously disappeared without a trace in the eighteenth century. I demonstrated how I chose important facts from my own reading about the ship, and I also modeled my writing. I brought in samples of my research, and as a class we would notice things about my writing and then make appropriate revisions accordingly. This modeling requires risk; writing and revising is messy business, so students saw me cross out old ideas and add new ones, and they watched as I drew arrows from words in the margins to the places they would fit into my writing. In short, they watched me struggle a bit, but they also saw me work through the struggle. Writing is about getting ideas on the page, and then knowing you can change your mind by adding, taking away, or rearranging. When students see us doing our own revisions, they can make choices about how to improve their own writing. Since my positive experiences with this modeling procedure two years ago, I have written every assignment I have asked my students to produce, and as part of my teaching I model how I revise these pieces.

Revising with a focus on word choice

As a first step to convincing my students that revising is important, I often convince them that it does not have to be difficult. One common instructional tool I use is to show a piece of my writing with weak verbs, and then ask students to help me change a few of the verbs so that they are stronger. Using model texts in context with memoir writing works well to serve this purpose. A memoir that has particularly strong verbs is *Fireflies* by Julie Brinckloe. In this first-person narrative, a young boy goes out to catch fireflies in jars with his friends. One page describes the fireflies blinking on and off while children in the neighborhood grasp at the fireflies and thrust them in jars. It is easy to act out this page, and point out to students that the actions are what make the piece memorable.

After reading this section of the book and discussing what we liked about the word choice, David Gonzales' fifth-grade class helped me with my piece of writing. Here is my original version of my story about getting in trouble one day with my brother and my neighbors:

My neighbors Tammy and Michael were out working in their yard, so my older brother Scott and I decided to help them. It was a really hot day. Michael, Tammy's older brother, pulled a rose and threw it at his sister. Then she pulled a rose and threw it at Michael. My brother Scott pulled a rose and threw it at me. Then I pulled a rose and threw it at him. Pretty soon there were no roses left on the rose bush.

The story goes on, with details about how we got in trouble for pulling all the roses off. Here is the revised paragraph, with suggestions from students to make my word choice stronger:

My neighbors Tammy and Michael were out working in their yard, so my older brother Scott and I decided to help them. We were sweating from the heat. Michael, Tammy's older brother, pulled a rose and threw it at his sister, and he cackled as hard as a hyena. Then she pulled a rose and threw it at Michael. My brother Scott hurled a rose at me. Then I pulled a rose and threw it at him. Pretty soon, we were shoving roses down each other's shirts, having the time of our lives until Michael and Tammy's mother came out and caught us.

The students helped me revise this piece in less than five minutes, and when I asked them to revise their pieces, they were ready. The modeling had proved to them that revision does not mean recopying; rather, it means rethinking what has been written and making some new choices.

Revising with a focus on "showing writing"

When students understand the concept that showing writing is strong writing, they can more easily find ways to improve their own writing. When we show through our writing, we are taking the reader with us by creating sensory images, or by specifically naming with the use of strong verbs and nouns. If I give one generic piece of advice to students regarding how to improve their writing, it is about adding showing details. I discuss how I introduce students to showing writing through acting exercises in Chapter 3, and I repeat these types of exercises as needed to remind students about how important it is to show rather than tell.

This advice about showing is good for all levels of writers, and in all types of writing. In a research project, for example, showing writing might entail adding specific dates or names of places. Without these important details, the focus of the project is unclear.

When writing a memoir, specific details including names of people and places are also important, and if the point is to make the reader feel part of the story, sensory images and the use of strong verbs are the details that make the reader relive the piece. When the technique of using showing writing is broken down into different categories, or a list of "Ways we can show in our writing," it becomes a powerful tool for revising existing writing.

Revising by taking away

In Neha Pall's and Shannon Damm's third-grade classrooms, the students had been writing about what they liked to do in their free time. The teachers had been working hard at helping students to add details to their writing. When I asked students what they knew about good writing, the list they created was impressive:

Good writing
- Has details
- Helps the reader to see
- Helps the reader to hear
- Helps the reader to taste or smell
- Helps the reader to feel
- Uses similes
- Describes
- Shows instead of tells

Clearly, these students had a sense of what good writing was all about. After looking at the writing about free time, the teachers noticed a number of students overdoing it: they added strings of adjectives in cases where one would have served the purpose, or they used similes that did not fit the purpose of the writing. I created a piece of writing that displayed some of the same problems to see what the students would notice:

> In my free time, I love to go swimming! When I jump in the icy, cold, chilly, freezing water, I immediately cool off. Splash fights can be fun if you are careful. Sometimes when I splash my friends, the waves look like humongous tornadoes spinning lightning storms out of the sky, destroying the whole entire universe! The best part of swimming is going off the high dive. Many people are afraid of heights, but I'm not! As I climb the towering stairs, my heart beats with excitement because I know the best part of the day is coming soon. I stand at the edge of the diving board, looking down into the water. Everyone looks like tiny fish swimming around. When I jump, I go super-duper, crazy fast, zooming like a squirrel chasing acorns in a tree! Hot summer days are best when you can jump in a nearby, refreshing pool.

I asked students if there were enough details. They agreed that I had enough details about what I liked to do in my free time. I asked them if I had too many details, and then gave them a few minutes to look at the writing again to see if I added unnecessary details to the writing. Volunteers came up and helped me improve the writing.

Jonathan crossed out "chilly" and "freezing." When I asked him why, he said, "Because you don't need all those words to show the water was cold."

Max crossed out "destroying the whole entire universe" because he said it didn't make sense.

Although many students liked the splashing waves being compared to tornadoes, Julie pointed out that tornadoes do not have anything to do with water. "You should say 'whirlpool.' Something with water."

The simile at the end of the piece, describing my speed going into the water as being "like a squirrel chasing acorns in a tree" did not fit, Hailey said, because squirrels don't need to chase acorns. Acorns can't run. She suggested "like a dog chasing a squirrel." John suggested something in the water: "like a shark chasing a dolphin," because the piece is about the water.

I was impressed with how quickly the students could improve the writing, and told them so.

Sharing revisions

"Now, watch what I do when I share my writing today," I told them. "Tell me what you think you are going to do after you have a chance to make your writing better.

"Before I revised, I wrote: 'icy, cold, chilly, freezing water' but I changed it to 'icy cold water.' I took out chilly and freezing because I already did a good job of describing the water with the words *icy* and *cold*."

I gave another example of a revision I made in my writing, and then explained why I revised it.

"Who can tell me what you are going to do today when you share?"

Several students raised their hands.

Cory said, "We are going to share what we changed, and then explain why we changed it."

I praised Cory, and then asked students to spend a few minutes revising their pieces. They used the list of what good writers do to determine if they needed to add anything, and they looked at the piece we revised together to see if they needed to take anything away.

I asked for volunteers to share their writing.

Armando shared his piece about his basketball team, and then said: "Before I changed, I wrote, 'I saw my great, good fantastic team exercising in the gym.' Then I changed it to 'I saw my fantastic team exercising in the warm basketball gym.'"

I asked him why he made the changes.

"Because I had too many words about my team. I didn't need all of them. But I wanted to say the gym was warm because it was cold outside."

I pointed out how Armando had effectively used revision in his piece:

"Armando did what writers do: he made choices about how to

make his writing better. He took out words in one place, and then he decided to add words in another place. Today, when you share, I want you to tell us what you changed in your writing to make it better."

Students love to share their writing, but sharing can become a learning experience for all students if they are encouraged to share for a specific reason. Armando helped the whole class by explaining why and how he revised his piece. Students can be motivated to revise if they know that they will be sharing their revisions with their classmates.

Revision circles

For many years, I have used Harvey Daniels' book *Literature Circles* as a resource for motivating students to have authentic discussions about books. Daniels and other experts in the field of reading have written much about the benefits of this approach to reading instruction.

When I asked students to share their writing, however, I often noticed that authentic discussions were not taking place. Students would comment on each other's pieces, but it was often hard to tell if they really *listened*, because the comments that followed were so generic: "I like the beginning," or "You made a good picture in my mind."

I decided to attempt to transfer the motivating parts of a literature circle into discussions about revisions in students' writing. I announced to my class they would be involved in a revision circle, and that when they shared their work, they would have to explain something they revised in their piece, and then ask for advice about what else they could revise. All members of the group would be engaged because they would have to think about how the revisions shared could help them with their own writing.

One reason I wanted to try this technique is because of my involvement in a few writer's workshops over the years. As part of the Denver Writing Project, I met with other writers in small groups for several weeks in the summer to share writing. Forming a group encouraged me to write: since everyone was bringing writing to share, I wanted to bring it as well. As the weeks went by, I realized that listening carefully to comments the group members made about someone else's writing helped me to improve my writing. I wanted to bring this same experience to my own classroom, so I developed a listening guide for students to fill out. On the paper, students are asked to think about how the discussion about one student's work can help them with their own work, as shown on page 84.

Prior to sharing their writing using this form, students must fill out what they wrote initially, what they changed, and why they changed it. They then have a purpose for sharing their writing. In addition, while other students share, each person writes down things they want to remember to try in their own writing. This paper is helpful because it becomes a record of a conversation. The students can be more independent in their revision discussions, and the teacher can walk around the room and monitor many groups at once.

In Julie Halfmann's fourth-grade class, students had written pieces describing ways to improve their classroom. She noticed that some of the students were not adding enough specific details to their writing, so we tried revision circles as a technique for helping them improve, and then discuss, their writing.

I first modeled my own piece about how to improve a classroom. I told them when I was their age, I always imagined having a water fountain in the room, and snacks anytime I wanted them. I wrote a short paragraph about my improvements, purposely leaving out specific details:

> I would make the classroom better by adding food and a drinking fountain. If we had snacks in the room, then we could eat something nutritious any time we wanted. If we had a water fountain, then we wouldn't have to go outside of the classroom to get drinks. Then we could pay more attention. I think it would be a good idea to make our classroom better by having snacks and water.

I asked students if they had ideas for helping me add specific details.

Mary suggested we add drinking fountains with fruit punch.

John recommended details about the type of food. When he suggested candy, I reminded him that we may want to stay with nutritious snacks, since this was school. We compromised by adding bananas, apples, and granola bars to my piece.

Revising My Writing

My name _____

   Share numbers 1, 2, and 3 with your group **after** you read your piece out loud.

1. This is what I wrote **before** I did my revision:

2. This is **how I changed my writing** in the revision:

3. I like my new writing better because:

   When other students in my group share, I will think about how I can make my own writing better.

   Here are **two things** I can try in my writing. I thought about these things while I was meeting with my group:

1.

2.

I asked students to look at their pieces to see if there was room for more details. After about ten minutes, I explained revision circles:

"In your groups, you are going to share one thing you changed in your writing today. First, you are going to use the form for revising to write down something you wrote before revising, and then how you changed it. Then you are going to record why you like your new writing better."

I modeled with my own writing:

"Before your help, I wrote 'we could eat something nutritious,' but I changed this by adding the details 'like bananas, apples, and granola bars.' I like my new writing better because I have used specific details."

Students spent a few minutes filling out their forms and then shared with table groups. Listeners were encouraged to take notes about how they could improve their writing.

Shawn did a good job of understanding the process. Prior to revision, he had written that he wanted the classroom to have a "floor that everyone could slide on." He changed this to: "A wax floor that everyone could glide on would be as slippery as ice." Based on the discussion in his group, he decided he could improve his piece by adding a simile and making more pictures in the readers' minds.

Using revision circles seemed to motivate this class to revise. They knew up front that they would be sharing original and revised pieces of their stories, so they wanted to be sure they made them better. I think that modeling is once again a key component here: using my own writing first helped all students feel they could then make their own writing better.

Revising to assess student growth

Kathryn Wells had asked her fifth graders to choose a favorite piece to revise. She felt that students would be more interested in using all the writing tools they had learned about during the year if they reworked a piece they were passionate about. When I visited Kathryn's class one spring day, I began by asking the students what they knew about revising. Their thoughts impressed me for two reasons: the students clearly know what writers do to make their pieces better, and they used their own unique voices to identify these qualities. I recorded their thoughts in the following list:

Revision Tools
Mrs. Wells' Class
Great lead
Interesting details through the whole piece
Showing writing, not telling writing, that makes a picture
Action verbs
End with a bang!
You-ish—write in your voice!
Sentence variety
Good word choice

I was particularly struck by the use of the term "you-ish," created by Kathryn's student Bryce, who clearly understood what it means to write with voice.

After identifying these tools, I read a piece to the students about my teaching experience in China. I asked them for feedback based on their list. They readily gave me a lot of advice, and felt I could add showing details by making a more clear picture in their minds of the English office at my school. They also recommended I use more action verbs. I followed this modeling by asking them to pick a section of their piece to revise. They could work with partners, or they could try using some tools on their own before they sought out a classmate's advice.

The next day, we met in revision circles. I first shared a section of my story from before and after it was revised, and asked Mrs. Wells to identify specifically what she noticed about the changes I made. She articulated clearly what she noticed, using the language in the list from the day before. This helped to focus students on what we would be asking them to do in their revision groups.

Tracey volunteered to allow her piece to be used as a student model after I finished talking about my piece. Her original version of a Cinderella tale, in which one of the stepsisters ends up being completely misunderstood, was full of humor and original details. But Tracey's passion for this piece helped her to find places to make it that much better. The changes made us laugh even more, and to make clearer pictures in our minds of how horribly Cinderella treated her stepsister.

When students shared their revised pieces in their small groups following Tracey's example, they used the revision circle model described above. Since they were already so grounded in the qualities of writing, and they chose their own pieces to revise, this exercise became the perfect tool for assessing student growth. All students, regardless of the quality of the original piece, found specific places to lift the level of their own writing, and they also gave clear feedback to their classmates.

Revising with English Language Learners

I have used the revision exercises described above in classrooms with English Language Learners. Revision for ELL students may be more on the word level than it is with students who are proficient in English, since students who are still learning the language have a more limited vocabulary. When we discuss using word choice for revising, I keep word banks of specific nouns, strong verbs, and descriptive adjectives up in the classroom for all students to use. Pictures can accompany these words to help students recall their meanings as needed.

The modeling of revision as described above is not only good practice, it is essential for students who are still learning the language. If they are to become successful writers, we must model very specifically what it is we want them to do. Even if it is difficult for an ELL student to revise, I believe in keeping them with the class during the entire writing process. This way, they will continue to be a part of the routines in the classroom, and as they acquire more language they will discover more and more ways to revise.

Final thoughts

When revision is used as part of the writing process, I think students feel more ownership of their writing. Sometimes, the first draft of a piece of writing ends up being stronger than a revised piece. But if I include revision as part of what we do when we write, then students can decide when to change something and when to keep it in its original form. I do not feel it is my place to always make that decision.

When students share their before and after pieces, as

described above, everyone benefits from the discussion about how to most effectively use the tools of a writer. All levels of writers can benefit from reworking a piece they care about, and there is no better motivator for revising than hearing a student share a piece that was great the first time, and then even better with some changes.

{ CHAPTER 7 }

How Do I Effectively Manage Writing Conferences?

Conferences are an integral part of teaching in the writing process classroom. When a teacher meets with a student writer, the learning can begin: the teacher can learn about the student as a writer, and the student can come away from the conference with ideas for how to improve his or her writing. But time often gets in the way of effective conferences. It can be difficult to schedule conferences with students, and to then adhere to the schedule. I have often planned to meet with students individually twice a month, only to find myself behind on my schedule in the first week. There have been times when I have met with students individually only once per month, and this has made me feel uncomfortable because I am not as aware of what students are working on as I would like to be.

My favorite resource for how to confer with students is Carl Anderson's *How's It Going?* He gives many suggestions for how to talk with students during conferences to help them as they seek to improve their writing. My purpose in this chapter is to discuss the organization of time during a conference, and how to manage the distractions that can often occur in even the most well-structured classroom.

Informal conferences: Checking the status of the class

One way I have managed to talk with more students about their writing is to rethink my idea of a conference. A conference can be one-on-one, in a space separated from the rest of the class, with the teacher listening to the student reading his or her work. Or, it can be more informal: as soon as writing time in my class begins, I used to do my own writing to model my writing process, and to show students that I, too, am a writer. I still do this periodically, but I more often will go around the room as soon as writing begins in order to see how things are going: to get a status of the class. Since I talk about my writing process often, and since I share my work with my students, I do feel I am modeling for them, even if I do most of my writing away from the classroom. Since one of my biggest concerns about conferences is finding the time to do them, I find it beneficial to immediately take a walk around the room once writing time has begun.

I often focus on students I have been concerned about, or students I have not met with for awhile. I will ask them a few questions about their writing, or about their ideas, and then I can possibly help them if they are stuck. This talk happens at their table or desk, while other students are writing. I bend down and ask these types of questions:

> "What are you working on?"
> "Do you have an idea for writing today?"
> If it is a revision cycle—"How are you going to improve
> your writing today?"
> If I have been concerned about the student not
> completing a particular piece—"Do you have a plan for
> finishing the piece?"

I take a few quick notes on a dated sticky note based on the student response, and then, later, when I confer with each child, I can check my notes to see if what we discussed was worked on, and I can begin my conference more efficiently. Even if a student has changed his mind about what to do with the writing based on my notes, the initial brief check-in gives me a place to begin. I tell students it is perfectly understandable that they may change their minds: writers do it all the time!

These more informal conferences can also be used to help all writers in the class. If I notice something a student is doing well, I can point it out to the rest of the class:

> "I am sorry to interrupt you, but I wanted to point out the strong verbs that Hannah is using in her work today. Listen while I read it to you, and then think about how you might want to go into your piece to make sure you are using strong verbs. Remember that we have been talking a lot about how verbs make writing more interesting for the reader."

Other teaching points that are being followed by students can be shared as an immediate model for reinforcement. I find this to be helpful, because the more that students become engaged in frequent rereading of their work, the more they believe writing is a process, not just a product.

How to make conferences more time-efficient

Setting a purpose for a conference can save a lot of time. Sometimes I ask students to set their own goals as writers prior to our conference. Then, I can read their pieces and goals prior to meeting with them, and I can be more focused on helping them find ways to rethink or improve, or celebrate, their pieces.

There are times when it is important to make suggestions to students about their writing. This can be tricky because writing is so personal. But if a class is grounded in the language of writing and writers, then it is easier to discuss ways to improve their writing. For example, if I know I want students to understand the power of specific nouns (Oreos vs. cookies, Ruffles vs. potato chips), then I need to make sure they understand that naming can improve their writing before I confer with them about it. I can bring in examples of professional or student writing to demonstrate how easy and effective it is to name people, places, and things in their writing. If I know I will be talking about effective use of similes, or the need for supporting ideas with specific details, this language of writing must not be introduced during a conference—it must be known by students prior to my meeting with them. Then, we are talking the same language, and the conference can proceed effectively. I still believe in the teachable moment—the time when the right advice comes at just the right time, even if an idea has not been discussed with the class. But when these magical moments happen in a conference, I use them as an example for the whole class so that I can maximize their potential for helping all students to improve their writing.

An example of a teachable moment happened for me one year when I was working with fifth graders. One of my students had a list of things she would like to bring to the beach on her perfect day. Typically, I warn students about using lists, because listing can lead to dull writing. But here was a list that was specific, and clear, and told so much about the writer. I shared it with the class, and said: "If you are going to list, then do it well! I won't say, 'Don't list' anymore—I will just say, 'Do it right!'"

The "whole-class" conference

There are times when I have found it useful to have a conference with one student while other students watch. While I talk with the student about his or her piece, I ask the students watching to think about how our discussion might help them as writers. This is the type of conference that requires the most careful setup for the teacher. It will only work if the students are engaged, and willing to believe they can learn from listening to the discussion about another student's piece. The student whose work is being discussed must also be comfortable with a careful examination of his or her writing in front of peers. I have had success in this approach when the piece of writing was strong, but not so strong that it was intimidating. I have also had success with this technique when the student whose work is being examined has the ability to reflect on why he or she might change a piece based on the conference.

I do not believe in substituting this whole-class conference for individual conferences, but my ultimate goal as an instructor is to help all of my students become as independent as possible. If I do not give them the opportunity to make their own decisions about their writing, and if they always rely on me for a conference prior to improving their writing, then I have not achieved my goal. By watching how one student thinks through a conference, I think all students can benefit if it is carefully orchestrated.

Stacking the deck—a technique for meeting with students in small groups for conferences

When I want to confer with my students about their writing, I often get frustrated because I have so little time. Although I firmly believe that the best way to impact student writing is to meet with each student individually, I have also realized that there isn't always enough time in the week to meet with each student.

I was wondering how to solve this dilemma one day when I thought about my reading groups. I felt I met the needs of many students when I met with them in small groups during reading time. I didn't meet with every student individually about their reading every week, and yet I still felt that I knew about them as readers. I wondered if I could somehow transfer the idea of meeting in small groups to writing conferences.

Although I still try to meet with students individually as often as I can, I have developed a technique I call "stacking the deck" that allows me to give students some individual attention within a small-group setting. Prior to conferring with students, I collect one sample of writing from each student. I read it in advance instead of having them read it to me. On a separate sheet of paper, I write each student's name. Then I write a specific praise comment such as "word choice" or "strong lead," and I take notes coded as stars on specifically what was good about the word or the lead. Then, I try to think of one content suggestion and one mechanics suggestion. These notes are coded with arrows. I might ask a student to add a few strong verbs, for example, and/or to check for correct sentences. The advantage to reading the piece in advance is that it saves time. I am not diminishing the importance of asking students to read their work aloud: I do this all the time during writing workshop, and as part of group and partner sharing. But if my goal is to help individual writers, I find it easier to read a piece in advance. I might ask them to choose a piece they really like, or to choose one they would like to make better so that they have more investment in this process.

Once I have read each piece and completed a coded list, I stack the papers so that all of the students who need more help will not end up working with me at the same time. The paper on the top of the stack is generally one that needs the most attention, followed by two or three that have only a few items for improvement. These papers are followed by another paper that needs more work, and so on.

I begin by praising the class for their work. As mentioned earlier, I often create a handout with examples from the class of strong writing so that we can talk about the strengths in the class before I start conferences. Then, I let them know that each one of them will be called up to talk with me, and during the time I am meeting with students, I expect them to be writing. They can work on a new piece or revise an old piece.

I call students up, one at a time, to a table in the front or back of the room. A table with a cutout for the teacher works well because it allows you to help more than one student at a time. I call my first student, one who needs to work quite a bit to improve his or her paper, to meet with me. I make sure this student sits close to me. Since I have my notes, I can give specific praise and specific suggestions. As soon as the student has begun making changes with a colored pen or pencil, I say that I am going to call someone else up, but that he or she should keep working. I ask the next student to come up and sit across from me. I again praise his or her good work, using my coded conference sheet, and then I ask the student to also improve the piece in a specific way. For a particularly strong writer, I may talk about what the student thinks he or she can do to improve the piece; in other words, I may leave it up to the student to choose what to do. While this student is working, I call up the third student. By the time I praise and then suggest an area to work on, the first student may be done. I can check with this student, and see how things are going while the other two work.

My goal is to allow students different amounts of time to complete revisions and error correction. Since not all writers need the same amount of revision, I do not ask each one to do the same thing. I often used this approach with one student at a time, but when I asked students to complete their revisions at their desks, they often didn't do it, or it took a long time. Some writers seemed to be clear about how to improve a piece, but when they went back to their desks, they didn't really know where to begin. By asking them to complete it at the time I make a suggestion, or at the time they come up with a way to improve their own writing, the revision and editing is more immediate. Because other students are at the table, no one is nervous because I am not watching over one student, waiting for him or her to revise.

A classroom example

I had worked with Jan Adair's fourth graders on narrative writing for several days, and it was time to confer. I read all of their pieces the night before my conferences with the students, and I stacked the papers so that I could meet with as many students as possible on my last day with them. During a forty-five-minute class period, I was able to talk with eighteen students. I used the method described above, calling students to meet with me at a table. Some stayed with me for thirty to forty minutes, while others either quickly finished, or went back to their seats to finish after our conference.

I called Niko first because I wanted to make sure he would have time to finish his story after he explained it to me orally. I also wanted to give him a chance to work on punctuation and sentence structure: he included very little punctuation in his story, and I wanted to see if he just needed a reminder, or if he might need some more direct instruction. Based on my notes, I was able to immediately praise Niko for the details he included in the beginning of his story:

"I like how you included the idea that the man is watching a scary movie in the beginning of the story, Niko! It makes me think something scary might happen to him!"

I quickly went to a question about content:

"I have a question for you: Why does the beast disappear at the end of the story?"

Niko responded: "Because the man scared him."

"That's a great detail! Do you think you could add that while I meet with someone else?"

Niko chose a green pen to make his additions to his story. This would allow me to quickly visually monitor his progress while I called the next student to the table.

Katie joined me next, while Niko worked.

"Katie, I loved your word choices! You use words like *squishy* and you describe Mrs. Allada's facial expressions! I can really make a picture in my mind! Good work! The part that I wonder about is at the end of the story. Did Mrs. Allada wonder how the animal got under the rug?"

Katie nodded.

"She does? Could you think of a way to include this in your story? I think it might make a better picture in my mind, just like you did in the rest of the story."

Katie took a purple pen, and worked on her additions.

Brett was next. He had not quite finished his story, but what he had completed had some strong word choices.

"Brett, I am so proud of your work here. You obviously know a lot about word choice. When you say *tiptoed*, I can just imagine your character carefully moving toward the lump under the rug, not wanting to make too much noise! And I love the simile you used: *slow as a turtle*. You are all set to finish your story. Do you think you can include some more details like the ones you already have been working on?"

Brett began his work with a purple pen, and I called the next student up to work with me. Niko ended up needing just a reminder about ending punctuation, and after Katie added some great details, she finished her story at her desk. I asked her to check in with me before the end of the period, which she did when there was a lull in my conversations with students at the table. Brett and I talked through the end of his story before he wrote so that he could think of some strong, specific details, and he ended up staying at the table for about ten minutes.

This process continued through the rest of the class, with some students spending a few minutes with me, and others spending more time. One thing I notice about this type of conference is that by the time many students meet with me, they have already revised their writing because of the mini-lesson prior to the conferences. If this happens, and I notice the changes, I ask them to tell me what they changed and why. This is a powerful way to reinforce the importance of revision, and to honor students as independent writers.

Keeping a focus

The technique described above may seem difficult to manage, but it actually has helped me to keep my writing instruction focused. When I read student papers, I am first looking for examples of strong writing from each student, which is motivating because I am looking for something positive. After that, I am reading to see what else I can teach my students, and to determine a general direction for instruction. I am able to individualize more for my students by organizing their papers in an order that won't overwhelm me or my students. By prioritizing need and knowing who may require more support, I am able to more effectively support all of my students.

Conferences with English Language Learners

A conference with an English Language Learner is an opportunity to learn more about how a student is internalizing the language. Sometimes, I am pleasantly surprised at how much ELL students are learning, especially if a student is shy and does not often share in front of the class. If I read pieces of writing in advance of a conference, I can determine if an ELL learner is able to communicate in writing. Unlike native speakers of English, I always try to have ELL students in a class read their work to me even if I have read it in advance, because this reinforcement of spoken English is very important as they learn the language. If I notice errors in grammar or usage and yet the content is clear, I follow the same procedure that I do with all students—I praise the content, and then help them with the conventions as they are ready:

> "In your story, you wrote, 'My dad bring me a new bike yesterday. I was so happy and I ride it all day.' This is great because I can tell you were very excited! Let me help you with some of your words. Since it happened yesterday, we would say 'My dad *brought* me a new bike yesterday.'

Do you know what I would say instead of 'I *ride* it all day'?"

If the student isn't sure how to work with tenses, a common problem for all learners of a new language, I take the opportunity to teach him or her during the conference. But if there are multiple tense errors, I will focus only on a few. My goal in the conference is to first praise, and then to guide, but to always keep students motivated to write more. If a conference becomes an exercise in recopying and correcting every error, then students will not want to produce much writing for fear of having to correct all of it.

Final thoughts

Managing time effectively is essential when trying to meet with students about their writing. Individual conferences, though ideal, are not always practical every week. But if I remember that I can learn a lot about my students in a short, informal talk, and if I try working with a few students at a time on their individual writing needs by reading the work in advance, then I can meet with more students, get a better feel for their progress, and more clearly identify the instructional steps I need to take.

An important factor in any conference is defining its purpose: if I just want to know what students are working on, a quick sweep around the room can accomplish this. If I want to know if students are internalizing how they revise, I can ask them to do their revisions in colored ink or colored pencil prior to meeting with them so that I can clearly see their changes. If I want to know how a student has progressed in learning English and getting ideas on the page, I need some individual time to sit and talk with this student. When my purpose is clear, I can be more clear as a teacher of writing, and conferences can become powerful tools for learning and teaching.

{ CHAPTER 8 }

How Do I Assess My Students' Writing?

Assessment is an important issue in education. We see more and more pressure placed on teachers to prove that their students are achieving at proficient levels in reading and math and, in my state of Colorado, in writing and science as well. State tests are not graded by the teachers who give them—by the people who know their students best—and yet these tests are pored over, and used to give grades to schools. Others are grading us on our performance, so the question of assessment is more important now than ever before.

Assessment of student writing is inherently difficult, both practically and philosophically. Reading student work is very time-consuming, and to assess it accurately, a second or even a third read is sometimes necessary. And if we believe that writing is a process, then isn't assessment anti-process because it doesn't honor the belief that we all continually grow as writers? Isn't writing process all about the journey, and assessment about a destination we can never truly reach? While I firmly believe in the writing process, I do not believe assessing student writing is anti-process. In fact, I now believe assessment is an important key to helping students become better writers. Before assessing any writing, the goal of the assessment must first be determined. Is the goal to inform instruction so that you will know how best to help your students? Or is the goal to give students feedback regarding their proficiency level? I believe the reason for assessing must be clear to both the teacher and the students in order for the experience to be valuable.

Assessment to inform instruction

Assessments that monitor student progress are important because without them, we cannot determine the effectiveness of our instruction. A collection of student work over time is needed to monitor progress in writing—a new assessment disconnected from what students have been doing in class is not necessary to determine if students have grown. I think assessing student work with the lens of wanting to learn more about how to proceed as an instructor fits very well into a writing process environment. I typically collect several pieces of writing from students every two to three weeks. I have set goals in mind prior to reading over their writing, but if one of my goals is to monitor progress, then I use the same rubric or scoring guide each time to mark student work. For example, I often begin the year with a strong focus on descriptive writing. If I want to monitor student growth in descriptive writing, then my scoring guide or rubric must address the elements of this genre. By scoring three or four pieces of student work produced at different times, I can determine whether or not students have grown. If they haven't, the use of a well-designed rubric will help to give me instructional tips. When I collect student work, I ask them to give me their best work to date. If they want to revise by crossing out and adding in other places, that's fine with me. They do not need to rewrite in order for me to get a picture of where they are as writers. Typically, students nervously ask me if I am going to grade their writing when I collect it, and I tell them the truth—I am very honest about my intentions whenever I read their work. I tell them that in order for me to be the best teacher I can be, I must collect work so that I know where we need to go next. If I am going to grade their writing with the goal of marking students on a range of proficiency levels, then I give them ample opportunity to work on their pieces before the grade is assigned.

An example of a four-point descriptive writing rubric I have used effectively in the past appears in Appendix D. I created it with the help of fifth-grade students, and because I wanted students to self-assess using the rubric, I wrote it in "student-friendly" language.

I have developed similar rubrics with second- through sixth-grade students. The key is to create a rubric that informs my instruction, and makes sense to students. I test the success of a rubric by how specifically it informs my instruction when I look at higher score descriptors. In the rubric above, if a student scores a 2, then I look to the descriptors in levels 3 and 4 for teaching points. A score of 2 tells me, and more importantly, tells the students, that better words could have been chosen, that sensory details can strengthen the piece, and that words should go beyond the use of "everyday" language. If students need specific ideas for how to add sensory details or unique ideas, I use excerpts of student work which has received a high mark. A simile, or a judicious use of personification, can be added as an example of how to go beyond everyday language. A sample of writing with sensory details can be used to show how the writer can appeal to the reader's senses.

Using assessment to inform instruction is clearly necessary if we want to monitor the progress of our students. When I use the word *assessment* in this context, I mean that I am using both formal and informal measures to monitor student progress and to inform my teaching. This is not easy work, but it is not as fraught with emotion as the idea of giving students a mark or a grade in their writing at the end of a term. Again, I think we must begin with looking at the purpose of the assessment.

Summative assessments

If my purpose is to give students a grade, or to give them a mark regarding their proficiency level in writing, the key is to have a body of evidence. Colorado relies on one test given over three days to determine student proficiency levels in writing, but I am still responsible for grading student work, and determining proficiency levels using my own judgment. We do not receive state testing information in time to score students at the end of the year anyway, so the data gathered from the state is not helpful if I must give students an end-of-year grade.

Grading is a tricky proposition. I often hear teachers and parents comment about the subjectivity of grading writing: it is not as clear-cut as math or reading comprehension because the student is producing something that is so unique, and so individual. I have worked on group scoring student work using common rubrics, and there are often differences of opinion regarding scores on writing. No matter how much we all agree on using the same rubric, which should establish clear guidelines for marking student work, there can still be disagreements.

There is no easy answer to this dilemma, so it is vital to have a body of student work to measure growth in writing. It is also important to score at least some of the work with a common rubric or set of criteria so that students can be compared to themselves. When I look at student scores on six or seven pieces of writing on a rubric that looks at ideas, style, and conventions, then I can get a fairly clear picture of their progress in writing. If the rubrics or criteria are created with student input, then we can all speak the same language when we discuss how much improvement they have made, and/or what they need to work on next.

A generic rubric that I have used effectively is loosely based on the rubric Colorado uses to score student writing. I have used it to determine students' grades in writing, and to determine proficiency levels. The rubric is found in Appendix E.

I weight the content and style scores more than skill scores because I feel it is important to focus as much as possible on the content of writing. I do not diminish the importance of grammar, but writing is a very complex task, and the main goal is to communicate clearly. In the "real world" of writing, the head of a company would not send out an important document without first sending it out for revisions, and then having it checked for grammatical errors. When I am looking at a body of student work, I have given them the opportunity to revise and to edit, but this doesn't mean the pieces will be perfect. When we score student work, I believe it is vital to separate content, style, and skills/conventions.

When I first started using the process approach to writing instruction, it seemed to take forever to get student work published. I never scored student writing until we had revised, and then revised again. I remember many times at parent-teacher conferences, twelve weeks into school, explaining to parents that I had no writing scores because we weren't quite done with final copies of any piece of writing yet. I had a lot of writing to share with parents, but all of it was in writer's notebooks, or in folders, and none of it was polished. I felt good about how fluent my students were becoming, but I didn't have enough information about how students were progressing in writing to please the parents. And, if I am honest with myself, I will admit I didn't have enough information for my own purposes either.

In recent years, I have decided that I must set deadlines for writing, and then stick with these deadlines. If I don't look at student writing regularly with an eye for how I can help students improve, then I cannot inform my instruction. By the time ten weeks of school has passed (a typical report card period in many of the schools I have worked in), I want to have enough information about student writing to give it a score on the report card, and, more importantly, I want information about what I still need to teach my students. I don't ask students to complete a final copy: I just ask them to give me examples of their best work so far. If they choose to word process their pieces, that is fine, and if they choose to look over their pieces and make revisions in pen or colored pencil, that is equally fine. I do want evidence that they looked again—that they revisited their chosen pieces, but I don't need them to publish in order to score their work.

If we observe our students carefully during writing time, and if we can quickly chart some of what we learn during conferences, we can collect much informal data about our students as writers. I always have a clipboard when I walk around the classroom, taking notes about things I notice. My notes used to be all narrative, but I started using some codes to help me assess even more students' progress as I walk around. For example, I might have the simple code of the letter *d* as an indicator that a student has demonstrated some strong descriptive writing. An *i* might mean a student successfully generates good ideas for writing. Conversely, I can code for concerns: I typically put a circled *sen* next to students' names when they are in need of extra work with sentences, or *cap* when they need work with capitalization. Circling these concerns makes them stand out from the non-circled codes which indicate students' strengths. The coding system doesn't matter—what matters is finding ways to know your writers.

One powerful result of charting and coding as I walk around the room is a visual reminder to me of who I have missed. If I have nothing by a student's name for several days, then I need to meet with the student. The charting process helps me to balance my time with students, so that I don't unfairly give all of my attention to only a few students.

Even with this most informal type of assessment, I let students know what I am doing:

> "I take quick notes or mark on a piece of paper either what we have talked about or what I notice in your writing. If you ever have any questions about what I notice, ask me! I would be happy to tell you what I notice about the work you are doing."

Careful observation is not just a tool for good writers, but for good teachers also.

Final thoughts

Assessing writing, and especially giving writing a letter grade, can go against the grain of what we most strongly believe in a writing classroom. Writing is about taking risks, and growing—it is not supposed to be about a single score which cannot possibly communicate all the amazing work students have created in a semester or a year. But if we save student work, and if we make them part of the process, and if we create rubrics and criteria in their language, then students can become more clear about how they can continue to improve as writers. If a body of evidence is used to help determine what instructional steps to take, then it can be easier to determine final proficiency levels. I believe an essential component of a writing classroom must be the teacher as researcher. This is the type of teacher who uses purposeful assessments to guide instruction as the students continue on their journey to become better and better writers.

{CHAPTER 9}

How Can I Prepare Students for Standardized Testing Without Compromising My Writing Program?

We live in an age of high stakes testing. In my state of Colorado, students are tested in grades 3 through 10 on reading and writing, and in math and science at some of the grades. The state testing program has become the one indicator of student performance that is used to measure the gains students are expected to make each year. This high stakes testing has created a lot of stress for teachers, but I think of it as a double-edged sword.

The tests have created more awareness of the need for strong writing instruction. While I do not advocate the use of standardized tests as the only measure of student growth, I do feel that our dialogues about instruction and how to help students improve have become more focused since the advent of testing. I have always worked with talented teachers and administrators, but the level of discussion about student work and how to help students of all abilities to grow has increased since the state tests came along. Now that the SAT includes a writing portion, the discussions about writing are becoming even more intense.

I worry that the tests have created the feeling that there are two types of writing: writing for a test, and then "real" writing. In other words, teachers often talk to me about how the requirement that students respond to a prompt on a test takes away their choice, and therefore does not reflect what writers really do. While I agree with this in part, I also feel that writers always have choices. The most talented writers in my fifth-grade class wrote beautifully on the standardized tests I had to give, and the writing did not look much different from the writing they produced for me on a regular basis. Students less comfortable with writing struggled on the tests, and their writing also did not differ from what they produced for me in class. Examining the released items scored by evaluators has proven to me that good writing is rewarded, even on standardized tests. The rubrics used for scoring are not the best scoring guides I have seen, but they do reward strong word choice, well-organized thoughts, and creativity. Yes, students must respond to a given prompt on standardized tests, but if they are grounded in the qualities of good writing, they are more likely to produce strong writing, even when responding to a prompt.

So, how can we help our students be prepared for standardized tests without compromising what we know about writing instruction?

Use writing to a prompt as a method of helping students improve their writing

I have generally been against the use of prompts during writing class. Students in my class might all be writing within a particular genre, but they had many choices about how to approach the genre as a writer. Although we might all be writing fictional stories, for example, the range of stories might vary from fantasy to historical fiction.

I have taken a number writing courses in the past three years, and I now feel a bit differently about how prompts can benefit writers. When I was part of the Denver Writing Project, we started every morning with some kind of prompted free write or quick-write: we were asked to write about a childhood memory, or we would choose a picture on a postcard to respond to. These were very open-ended writing activities, but they were prompted in the sense that we were given something to start from. I also have taken poetry and fiction writing workshops, and nearly every one of my classes began with some kind of idea to jump-start our writing. We were warming up, practicing our craft. Books on writing craft are full of ideas to get the words flowing, and I see these as a form of prompted writing. What I learned from taking these courses and going through exercises in writing books is that I often produced writing I was proud to share. One of the best pieces of writing I developed stemmed from a ten-minute quick-write during the Denver Writing Project. As participants in the workshop, we all received a postcard-sized photo one day. Mine featured a camel in the desert. I wrote a very short story about a woman who realized, while on the back of a camel in the Gobi desert, that she needed to leave her husband. I don't know where the idea came from, but the picture prompted me to write. This type of exercise, and others like it, has convinced me that introducing an idea for writing does not equate to lifeless products from students.

I see my role in helping students get ready for tests as being no different from what my instructors were trying to do for me in writing courses: the central goal is to improve writing. Exercise helps.

An example of a prompt assignment focused on strong writing

Hank Wotli was concerned that his fourth graders were not writing with enough voice. He also wanted students to practice responding to a prompt. I began the lesson with two prompt-response examples from students. Both were well written, but one had far more specific details than the other. I frequently save student work from year to year and take student names off when doing this type of exercise. I am very careful to never share a bad example of student writing: I only share well-written examples, though I often look for more advanced pieces to compare with average pieces.

After asking students to read each piece, we made a list together about the qualities they liked in each piece. The students picked specific words, phrases, and sentences, and then told me what they noticed. I wrote this on the chalkboard:

Good writers
1. Write using their senses (seeing, hearing, touching, tasting, smelling)
2. Use similes
3. Use strong words that not everyone would think of
4. Use good verbs

For each one of the items, students were able to identify one or more examples in the very strong piece, and a few examples in the average piece. I asked them to add one detail to the average piece, using the criteria they developed. I told them:

> "Since we know what good writing looks like, find one place where we can make one of the pieces better. Use one of the techniques we discussed, and when we share, identify what you did as a good writer to make the piece even better."

This part of the lesson only took a few minutes. I allowed students to work in pairs, and I left some examples of strong verbs, similes, and sensory writing on the chalkboard as a reference.

It was now time to write original pieces. I asked students to write about their favorite food using some of the techniques they had listed on the board. I wanted them to keep these techniques in mind consciously *while they were writing*. As a rehearsal, I asked them to join a partner, and while talking about a favorite food, to purposely use the strategies listed on the board. Each partner was given thirty seconds to talk about a favorite food, and then I asked several students to share what technique they had used in their verbal rehearsal. I pointed out examples of voice as students shared aloud. I defined voice as coming up with a way of saying or writing something that only you might think about. This verbal rehearsal allowed me to determine if my ELL students would struggle. I let them know they could use their native language if it was easier, but I also monitored the ELL students' rehearsal to see if they had trouble coming up with enough words. As the writing begins, I always monitor the progress of all the writers in the room, watching to see if anyone needs some words written on the board, or more verbal rehearsal prior to actually writing.

As students finished their writing, I asked them to make a checklist numbered 1 through 4 on the side of the page. The numbers refer to the qualities of good writing they developed while reading writing from other students. Each quality is assigned a number, and I asked students to put a check mark by each item for which they have a strong example. If they couldn't mark each item, then I encouraged them to go back and add that quality to their writing.

Katie checked off all four items from the list on the board, and then shared her piece with the class:

When my mom orders fried rice, I feel very enthusiastic. Finally, the juicy, steamy fried rice. I race to the door like a cheetah at its fastest. I spring to them and, snatch the fried rice, and start inhaling the rice. I could eat it morning, afternoon, and night, even for snacks if I could. After one day of Chinese, there's always tomorrow.

When Katie shared her piece aloud, she was able to point out her examples of strong writing, making it very clear to us all that she knew the qualities of well-crafted text.

Chelsea wrote about chicken, and also felt that she included the qualities of good writing in her piece:

I love chicken. If it was up to me, I would eat chicken every day. When my grandma buys KFC I race my sister because I can smell that chicken. Then I sit down to gobble down tender, juicy, spicy chicken. I put honey on my biscuits and gravy on my potatoes. And I grub. It's so good, I feel like I'm in heavenly heaven. I was the last person at the table scarfing down the chicken. It was the bomb!

Chelsea was also able to discuss with the class her use of strong writing, and I could used examples from both students' writing to talk about how they used voice to write well. Each piece is clearly written by someone who is enthusiastic about the food she loves, and the voice of each student comes through loud and clear.

This is an example of a lesson based on a prompt. Students were asked to write about a food they loved for about ten minutes at the end of the lesson. But because I framed our discussion around the qualities of strong writing, I feel I was helping each student to become a better writer. Good writers think about strong verbs, and word choices not everyone would think of. Writers try to find a place to add sensory details, and they use similes when appropriate. These qualities of writing appear in the rubric that students' work will be measured against, and these qualities also appear in the state of Colorado Language Arts Standards, which align closely with the national standards. But the qualities transcend tests, rubrics, and standards, for these same traits exist in all good writing, whether it appears in stories, magazines, newspapers, or novels. Whether writing to a prompt or writing from passion and choice, student writing should reflect these qualities.

Keeping the needs of the students in mind

The lesson described above grew from a need identified by a teacher in a class: students were not writing with enough voice. I used the prompted writing examples of voice because the teacher also wanted to focus on helping students to become better at writing to prompts. The whole lesson took approximately one hour, and by the end, all students had examples of strong writing they could share based on criteria they developed. As soon as a few students shared, it became clear that choice is inherent in any writing, even prompts: very few students chose the same food to write about, and all of them used their own word choices, and their own voices, to write about a food they loved.

I do not advocate using prompts as a focus for writing instruction. I believe that students should be given choice, and that we should talk with our students about their goals as writers. But I do believe that with the methods described above we can keep our instructional focus for writing on solid, process-oriented ground by not completely separating writing on a test from what we know about good writing.

The issue of time

Good writing can take a lot of time, and a lot of revising, and this is where the testing issue most goes against what I believe about writing instruction. Students are expected to create a well-written piece in a relatively short time on standardized tests. If students are stuck for long, they won't finish, and the resulting scores will not reflect their abilities as writers.

I think there are many strategies for helping students through the time limitations. In the lesson mentioned above, students first examined writing, identified qualities they liked, tried out some of the things good writers do on a piece that was already written, verbally rehearsed their own writing, wrote, and then shared. The writing part took only about ten minutes. Not everyone produced a full paragraph, but the majority of the class produced about half a page of well-written expository text. This reminds me of the prompt exercises I mentioned earlier: in many writing workshops and classes I have taken, the class begins with a ten-minute quick-write. I didn't always feel that I produced a strong piece of writing during these exercises, but when I did, I was pleasantly surprised that I produced anything at all worth sharing in only ten minutes. These exercises were often followed with a quick revision idea, and we were given another few minutes to examine our writing and improve it based on a revision tool. So in twelve minutes, I could produce something worth sharing. If this built my confidence as an adult, then I think it can also build the confidence of students.

Writing practice exercises lasting for ten minutes can help students build confidence. They aren't stuck for topics if we give them an idea to write about, and if they are able to produce something they want to share in this short amount of time, then they start to believe they can write. I have heard many professional writers speak about their process, and they often talk about how they may labor over several sentences in a story, but at other times, the writing just "happens." It is the practice of writing that all of these writers mention. Students can have good writing "happen" if we provide opportunities for this best of moments, when the right word just comes to mind.

At the end of Katie's piece about Chinese food above, she writes, "After one day of Chinese, there's always tomorrow." I praised her for coming up with such an interesting concluding statement for her piece. When I asked her how she thought of it, she said, "I don't know—it just popped in my head." It was not the prompt that created this situation, but rather our discussion about the writing. In other words, we do not have to rely on prompts to create moments of revelation for our students, but if we use even standardized test practice as an opportunity to discuss what writers do, then the students will become more aware of their own writing process.

Prompt writing in the primary grades

In Colorado, third grade is the first year for standardized writing tests. This causes much anxiety for third-grade teachers, and the stress has manifested itself in second grade as well. Primary teachers want to support their colleagues, so they often decide to prepare students for what is to come by practicing prompts.

I have worked with teachers who make practice in prompt writing part of their writing classrooms, by using it as just another way of helping students become better writers. I worked with Karen Sundling's class at Antelope Ridge, and she wanted to see how students would respond to practicing a prompt with me.

I avoided calling our work "test practice," and I grounded our discussion of what we were about to do in terms of what writers do: they come up with ideas, and they think of how to write them, and then they use the best possible words while they write.

I followed a very similar format to the lesson described earlier: I had saved some writing second graders produced, which described their bedrooms and how they would change them if they could. We examined two pieces, and decided together that the stronger of the two pieces had words that made pictures in our minds, gave the reader details, and used similes. I asked them to picture their rooms in their minds, and then to think about what they wanted to change in their rooms. They rehearsed verbally first, I modeled my own thinking and writing for a few minutes, and then they wrote. We allowed about fifteen minutes, with time built in for those who wanted to draw their rooms prior to writing. Students were ready to write by the time their pencils hit the page, and many of them produced strong writing within the time frame. An excerpt from Shahbaaz's piece demonstrates his understanding of how to add specific details. His room included the following features:

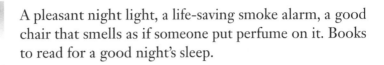

A pleasant night light, a life-saving smoke alarm, a good chair that smells as if someone put perfume on it. Books to read for a good night's sleep.

As is typical in some classrooms when similes are mentioned, some students used multiple similes in a short piece. Brooke is doing the job of a writer—she is practicing her craft—in the following excerpt about her room:

My bedroom is as purple as grapes! I have a squishie pillow as soft as velvet! I have a bunk bed as white as snow!

These students explored an idea in the context of a writer's workshop: though they were given an idea to write about, the lesson began with a discussion about what writers do to make readers want to know more. Then, after drafting some ideas aloud, and drawing, if needed, to visualize prior to writing, students worked on their pieces. They each included details unique to them, and in some cases their personalities shone through, loud and clear. Katie had this to say about her dream bedroom:

I wish I had a Spongebob TV with a Spongebob remote control and a little couch. I also wish that my room wasn't sooo messy. It would be a lot cleaner and fun. I always wish that would happen. Soon. Really soon. Super dooper soon!

Students enjoyed sharing these pieces with their classmates because they felt successful as writers. Even though one of our goals in this particular lesson was to see how well students would respond to an idea they were asked to write about, we followed a process approach to instruction, and we were pleased with the results.

The importance of modeling

In addition to asking students to periodically practice prompted writing to get ready for testing situations, I often model writing to a prompt. I ask them to give me a topic, and then I spend five or ten minutes writing, recording my thoughts on the overhead or on chart paper while thinking aloud. It is important to think aloud during this process because then students can hear what I think as a writer. I keep a list of qualities of good writing nearby, so that they can see that I refer to them often. It is always a risk to write in front of students, but I can't imagine not doing it now that I model for them so often. If we are going to model good reading, and good math work, we must also model good writing. I often do not produce my best writing when I model for students without advance warning, but I am getting better, and I always think about what makes writing strong as I write. The fact that I am getting better at writing on demand in front of students after a lot of practice proves to me again that practice is what will help students the most as they get ready for testing.

Test practice: How often?

When I last taught fifth grade, I didn't want to burn students out on practicing for tests, so I made a calendar in my plan book and marked about ten different days when I would complete a prompted activity similar to the one described earlier in this chapter. When I asked students to practice by writing to a prompt, I planned my instruction based on their needs. So, if I noticed they were not using strong verbs, I would find some student writing with strong verbs, examine it, and then model my own writing process to a prompt that would lend itself to strong verb choices. I would ask students to help me identify the strong verbs in my own writing, or to help me to change weaker verbs to stronger verbs. After a verbal rehearsal, students would complete their own writing. By spreading this practice out during the year, students didn't get burned out, and they also connected it to their own writing because I was working on a craft I noticed they needed to improve. The writing was not divorced from what we were already doing in class.

One of the most successful techniques I have used to help students monitor their own progress in writing was given to me by a master teacher named Steve Johnson. After students respond to a prompt, and after they have had a chance to determine how well they performed based on criteria we have created as a class, I collect each student's writing and assign it a random number. I don't want students to be able to identify who has created the piece of writing, so I ask them to leave their names off, and I put a number on it. Then, I hand out papers to groups of four students, making sure that each group has no student papers from group members. Each group member is given four sticky notes, and they record on the note which qualities from the criteria that the class established are found in the writing pieces. Only positive comments are allowed on each paper. I then ask the groups to choose one paper they would like to share aloud with the class as an example of a piece that uses many or all of the qualities of good writing. We end this part of the lesson by sharing aloud one paper from each grouping. This process creates ownership for students: they are determining what works in each piece, and they know they will get their own paper back with specific qualities of good writing recorded on sticky notes. The process is positive: everyone is praised, and the pieces shared aloud are written by fellow classmates, which reinforces my belief that the best models of writing can come from students themselves. The only problem I have had with this approach has stemmed from the fact that some students do not write legibly. If their writing cannot be read due to handwriting, I normally take the paper out of the initial stacks, and talk with the student about it. If students complain that they cannot read an illegible paper, then it has sometimes motivated the student who produced the paper to be more careful about writing.

Students may feel they are left out of this process if their paper is not shared aloud by the group. There are a few ways I have used to honor each piece in the class. One way is to ask the students in the group to read one or two sentences of strong writing from every paper. Then, I collect the papers and read a few aloud the next day in full, so they can hear how a piece flows. I can also do the opposite: I can ask groups to share a completed piece, and then I can lift one or two sentences from each piece that was not shared and bring those to class the next day as further examples of good writing.

When students are encouraged to identify strong writing in their classmates' papers, it creates an environment where writers are mining each other's work for elements to praise rather than pick apart. I feel very strongly that students can help each other become better writers, but in order to build the trust of everyone in the class, I often ask them to focus only on the positive examples of strong writing they notice in each other's pieces.

Grammar instruction

I include the discussion of grammar in the larger question of testing because a large portion of a student's writing score on the state assessment in Colorado is based on knowledge of grammar. The issue of grammar is also important to discuss in the context of the writing-process classroom because it is something we all worry about, even when we have the best of intentions. Misspellings, capitalization errors, and poor sentence structure often pop out when we read student writing, overwhelming our ability to actually "see" the content. Teachers notice errors in student work, and they become frustrated because they have worked with students on the conventions of language. They feel that students should transfer this knowledge regularly to their writing.

I, too, used to be very frustrated with my students when they would make errors in their writing. I would complete a two-week unit on the sentence, only to find my fifth graders still writing in fragments and run-ons. Is it possible to have the best of both worlds? Can we hold students accountable for conventions, help them get ready for grammar questions on mandated tests, and still nourish their creativity in a process-oriented classroom?

This is a complicated issue. There are no simple solutions, but it has been proven through research such as Constance Weaver's *Teaching Grammar in Context* that grammar exercises out of context do not improve student writing. Since this is true, I think the place to start is with each student. We must try to find a way to consider the individual needs of the students without feeling the need to create dozens of individualized plans. The process of helping students with conventions must be doable, or we will just remain frustrated.

When I look at student writing to develop ideas for a direction for instruction in conventions, I keep a few basic questions in mind:

Developing a set of realistic grammar and mechanics expectations for your students

> Do the students in general have a
>   sense of sentence structure?
> Do they have a command of punctuation and
>   capitalization rules?
> If there are spelling errors, can I still read the words they
>   were trying to spell?

For me, these questions create a hierarchy. I concern myself first with sentences, and then capitalization/punctuation, and finally with spelling. When I do this, it allows me to not panic about everything at once. My first step when I focus on conventions is to look at sentences. If I notice that a number of students are having difficulty producing correct sentences, then I hand back the student work, and I first praise them for the work they have done. I generally will lift some strong writing from the class and make copies for everyone to examine. I want to preface any discussion about conventions with a focus on good writing. By reading in advance for strong writing, I can create a handout with examples from the class to prove to them that they are writers. Once I praise and reinforce the strong content from the class, I am ready to talk about conventions.

After the students have their papers back, I hand out colored pens or pencils. I generally use blue, green, or purple—red has too much of a negative connotation. I then ask students to check for sentence and capitalization errors in their pieces:

> "Find your sentences by marking periods"
>   and
> "Find the places where you need to add capital letters."

Notice that working on sentences, which is first in my hierarchy of conventions, also includes a focus on capitalization and punctuation. I often model a quick correction of a sentence I have written on the overhead or chalkboard to demonstrate that I do not want students to erase. If students do not have errors, then I ask them to write, "No Errors" at the top of the page in color. I generally allow about five minutes for this. My purpose is to accurately inform my instruction. If even a few students can find their sentence errors in this five-minute time frame, then I know these students do not need more direct instruction in sentence structure: they just need a reminder. The students who are not able to identify their errors, or who change their sentences incorrectly, will become a group I can instruct further. Depending on the size of this group, I can work with them as part of my guided instruction in the course of the day.

I have abandoned the idea of using sentence worksheets because I was not seeing direct translation into student writing. If I can determine exactly who needs more instruction in sentence construction by using the method above, then I can pull this group of students and go through some of their writing, sentence by sentence, individually, to understand what students are thinking. Sometimes the problem of incorrect sentences is easy to solve, and sometimes it isn't. Requiring everyone in a class to complete conventions worksheets makes no sense when everyone does not have the same difficulties. But asking them to find their errors and correct them before I look at the papers again separates my class into three groups: those who consistently write correctly, those who need reminders, and those who need some more direct instruction.

As a rule, I quietly remind all students of sentence structure, capitalization, and punctuation as I walk around the room examining student work. I try to encourage students to think a bit about conventions as they write so that they do not have to go back and fix too many things at the end of a page. Obviously, I differentiate this depending on the needs of the students, but I want to make sure that as many things are correct as possible before I read the work.

I use the same technique mentioned above for capitalization, punctuation, and spelling. I hand out colored pens or pencils after I have read the work, I quickly model a correction in my own writing, and then I ask the students to spend a few minutes trying to identify and correct their own errors. If they think they have a spelling error, but are not able to correct it, I ask them to circle the word they believe they have misspelled. When I do this often enough, and look for patterns of error, I can find teaching points for those students who have a hard time with spelling. Again, I can differentiate for these students: while they are writing, if they know they cannot spell a word, I ask them to approximate the spelling, and to move on with their writing, but to mark that line with a quick check mark so that they remember to go back and check their spelling at the end of the writing time. This reinforcement of expecting students to become independent editors eventually helps most of my students improve in their skills. These ideas are not uniquely my own: I have worked with teachers who have used similar ideas with their classes, with students of varying needs. And, I have seen these same students greatly improve in the content, style, and conventions of their writing. I have also seen these same students approach grammar sections on state tests with more confidence. In a process-oriented classroom, it does not need to be either–or: we help students to be more careful writers even as we encourage them to be more passionate about what they are writing.

Testing and ELL students

I have used the techniques mentioned above in classrooms with ELL students. I always leave an example of some good writing on the chalkboard or chart paper to look at as a model, or I may even help an ELL student get started by helping with the first few sentences. The models used to produce the criteria list help students to understand what type of writing we are discussing. I include visual cues to represent the qualities of the good writing. For example, if sensory details are mentioned, then I sketch an eye for "seeing details" and an ear for "hearing details." If strong verbs are mentioned as a quality of good writing, then I ask students to act out the verbs, so that everyone can make a clear picture of what the verb actually means.

The verbal rehearsal is a key element in practicing for writing to a prompt. I encourage the ELL students who have mastered some English to be part of the verbal rehearsal, because when a partner practices a prompt out loud, it can help the ELL students continue to acquire more language. If the ELL students have enough language to say only some of the words they want to say in English, but they are literate in their own language and can write to the prompt, then I encourage them to write in their native language. If they are limited in English, and are not quite clear on the purpose for writing outlined in the prompt, then I still try to get them to produce something on the page: a picture of a favorite food, for example, or a drawing of a place they have visited. With enough picture cues and a list of vocabulary left on the board, I can normally help all ELL students produce some writing that creates meaning. I insist they remain with the group and stay with the process, because then as they acquire more language they will already have mastered the routines of the writing classroom.

The ideas for grammar in context mentioned above also work well with ELL students. ELL students are more likely to make errors in subject-verb agreement than native-English-speaking students, and they are more likely to use words that do not quite carry the exact meaning they are trying to convey. But if I look carefully at their writing, and make my decisions for instruction based on who needs reminders and who needs direct intervention, I find myself being more successful with all students. Sentence structures in English are quite complicated when compared with many other languages, but the more that ELL students are exposed to the language, and the more they try it out, both verbally and in writing, the better chance they have of becoming successful.

When I first started working with ELL students and assumed writing was too complex for them, I asked them to work on the computer, or some fill-in-the-blank worksheets instead. But my expectations were not high enough. Many master teachers I have observed since my first days of working with ELL students have convinced me that it is important that all students take part in the classroom rituals for each subject. When all students are included, I am sending a strong message about the importance of creating a learning community.

Final thoughts

Do we have to abandon best practices in writing instruction when testing time nears? I don't believe we do. Good writing is good writing, and we can help our students be ready for anything by building their confidence as writers. If choice and tools for improvement are at the core of an approach to writing instruction, I believe our students can take a test with confidence. Even when writing to a required test prompt, students should feel empowered because they can make choices about specifics to include, and they can choose the tools they will use as they craft their responses. As teachers, we have no control over the uses of testing information, or the fact that it is often just one test that measures a school district's progress. But we do have control over how we use our instructional time. Our goal should be to help students become the best writers they can be, so that when they are met with any writing challenge, they can approach it with confidence.

CHAPTER 10

How do I Plan for Writing Instruction?

I have read many books on writing instruction, and all of them tend to give similar advice about planning: set aside approximately an hour a day for writing instruction, and meet weekly in individual conferences with students. This is very sound advice, and I have used it effectively. But, what about when things do not go as planned? What about those days when many students are absent, or when the third assembly of the week interrupts the schedule, and then state testing eats time out of three weeks of school? Scheduling time for the writing block should begin with determining the amount of time being planned for: are you planning for a year, for a unit of study, for a week, or for a day? Some suggestions for how to think about these different time blocks follow.

Planning for a year

If certain units of study are going to be followed through the course of a year based on state, district, or school guidelines, setting deadlines for these units of study can be helpful when planning instruction.

For example, for many years when I taught fifth and sixth graders, my teammates and I ended the year with a unit that required students to create their own magazine. This project required students to use all of the writing strategies they had been working on all year, and the open-ended assignment allowed for maximum choice while still providing a tool for determining how much students had grown in the year. The magazine became a sort of community celebration as it continued over the years, and families looked forward to seeing what their students would create during this project. Since the magazine took approximately five weeks to complete, and it was one form of summative assessment, we placed it at the end of the school year. We worked backward from there, fitting in units that included research, narrative, memoir, and technical writing.

As we planned for the year, we noticed when we could fit writing in across the curriculum. For example, we could do a research unit closely connected to social studies topics. Students had a choice of what they wanted to research, but we connected it to our American history standards. Technical writing in the form of lab reports could happen in science class. Writing did not have to exist just in the domain of language arts, so if there were days when we would have to shorten our language arts block, we could plan accordingly and make sure to have writing happen in science or social studies. Writing in other content areas is not only a good idea in terms of planning and scheduling, but I think it is also good for students. Many of my reluctant writers in the past have loved science, and they were more than willing to write in the context of their favorite subject. They may have reluctantly completed a memoir, but then enthusiastically explained their thinking in science class.

Planning for a year is an excellent way to think backwards: once my teammates and I decided which type of writing would occur in each month, we could begin gathering our resources and planning for instruction. We knew what types of writing we would need to cover in order for students to be successful in each unit. Though we knew we would have to adapt our ideas according to student need, having the plan created a strong scope and sequence that covered the requirements of our district curriculum. Organizing for the year ensured that we would give students ample opportunity to demonstrate their growth in writing.

An example of a yearlong plan is found in Appendix F.

Planning for a unit of study

Writing units can last for various blocks of time, depending on the complexity of the writing and the prior knowledge students bring to your class. I have taught units lasting for as long as five weeks, as in the magazine project mentioned above, and for as short as a few days, but regardless of how long the unit is, certain key elements have made the organizing of my time more effective. I need to make sure students have time to examine models of what they are going to write, to rehearse or practice, to revise their writing, and then to celebrate or publish their writing.

I have successfully organized the steps mentioned above in short time blocks when I am asking students to produce either very short pieces or when we are working on a type of writing they know a lot about. As I mentioned in the first chapter, I typically begin my year with a focus on descriptive writing. If I want students to write about special places, then I show them a model of good writing that describes a place. I use an excerpt from a novel, or a short picture book, and we examine the writer's craft. After identifying the elements of the descriptive piece, students can verbally rehearse what they might write about a place that is special to them. They can bring in photos of a place they love to help them develop their ideas. Once they rehearse, they can try out their ideas in writing, and then we can celebrate with a group share. I know up front in my planning that this is just one type of descriptive writing, and that it is part of a larger unit of study. But, I still organize the writing block with the key elements of modeling, establishing criteria, rehearsal, writing, revision, and celebration, so that students feel a sense of accomplishment and I have information for instruction. In the larger blocks of time for an entire research unit, or the magazine project, I keep the same elements, but each part lasts longer, and the writing produced by students is longer.

Planning for a week

If I have established units of study for the year, and then identified blocks of time for each unit, I can look at a typical week and plan my writing time accordingly.

In a typical week in the many schools I have worked in, I have rarely had my entire class for a solid language arts block all five days of the week. I had students pulled for enrichment or support, but not always at the same time on the same days. I might have five students leave twice a week, and four different students leave three or four times a week. This made it difficult to find time when my whole class was together. I tried to work on my schedule so that I could have at least three uninterrupted hours with my entire class for writing each week. A typical weekly schedule is listed below as an example of how I fit in my writing time.

Monday, Wednesday, Friday
8:30–9:00   Writing, whole class
9:00–10:15   Math
10:15–11:00 Specials
11:00–12:15 Reading (two pull-out groups leave)
12:15–1:00   Lunch
Afternoon   Social studies and Science

Tuesday, Thursday
8:30–9:00   Reading
9:00–10:15   Math
10:15–11:00 Specials
11:00–12:15 Writing, whole class (no pull-out groups)
Afternoon   Social studies and Science

This schedule allowed for a solid hour of daily reading instruction or writing instruction, but not both. I felt it was important to include all students in the writing block, so I shortened the block to thirty minutes when pull-out groups happened on Monday, Wednesday, and Friday. Since the pull-out groups focused on reading instruction, I worked on reading when they were out of the room.

As I noted in the section on planning for the year, my teammates and I were committed to including reading and writing strategies in science and social studies. We had a science fair early in the year, so students were involved in a lot of authentic writing: they recorded observations, created hypotheses, and drew conclusions about their data. We used the elements of a writer's workshop as students experimented: they rehearsed what they wanted to write through discussions with classmates, they drafted their ideas, met in revising groups, and created posters to display their findings as a way to celebrate. Even if I only had thirty minutes of writing time during language arts with my whole group earlier in the day, students were often writing during other parts of the day. When organizing for writing in the context of a week, I think it is important to keep track of writing that is done in other subject areas. A strong writing program can be delivered in multiple subjects.

Planning for a day

Let's imagine the worst-case scenario:

You arrive at school, ready for the day. You have planned a great revision lesson for the students, and have set time aside for the whole class to try out some revisions in their own work, and then to meet with a small group to share their thinking. At the end of the writing block, you plan to ask students to share what they learned about revising, and to give examples from their own work to clarify their thinking.

As soon as the day begins, the schedule is interrupted with a fire drill. The first fifteen minutes of the day are lost, and you have to take some time out of writing to finish up the math lesson you had begun prior to the fire drill. Then, just when you are ready to begin the writing class, your teammate tells you the guest speaker for social studies has made a mistake and arrived a day early. Can you please flex and let the person speak during the language arts block? The rest of the morning is devoted to the speaker, and then the afternoon is full of science and social studies. I know this is not something that happens every day, but, can at least some writing instruction still happen?

If I was planning a lesson on revision, I might spend five to ten minutes to prep the students for the longer lesson that will happen later—perhaps the next day. I can grab a well-written book, and ask the students to identify the crafts an author uses as they listen to me read aloud. Or, I can quickly write a dull, "telling sentence" on the board, and challenge them to revise it so that it is full of descriptive language and strong verbs. As we walk down the hall to specials or that assembly, I can ask students to raise their hands when they can verbalize a descriptive phrase for something they notice in the halls that they never noticed before. After specials or the assembly, I can ask the class to share what happened in music or art, first with a telling statement, and then with a revised, descriptive, "showing" statement. These quick exercises will help to ground the students in the work I was hoping to accomplish in a well-executed, hourlong lesson. But outside factors got in the way, so I had to improvise. I think when we organize for a day, we must remember that not everything goes as planned. We can still keep our objectives in mind, however, regardless of the interruptions: thinking back to that pesky fire drill, what about giving students two minutes in six small groups to come up with brilliantly descriptive sensory details about this experience, and then ask each group to share in one minute? This would take only about eight minutes: two minutes to plan, and then about six minutes to share. I try to take advantage of every learning opportunity when I work with my students, knowing that the schedule is not always in my control.

Maintaining flexibility

I have worked in four different schools, each with its own personality regarding scheduling and the day-to-day workings of a school. In one of these schools, math was the subject that could never be rescheduled because students might go to a different grade level for math instruction depending on their needs. A first grader who needed more advanced math, for example, would go to a second-grade classroom. Our math time was set for seventy-five minutes each day, with no exceptions. Assemblies and field trips were planned accordingly, so when a curricular area was impacted, it was not math.

I worked in another school where we had frequent assemblies, which normally occurred in the morning. Because of the number of pull-out groups I had that year, this often impacted my language arts instruction. This made it difficult to fit in an hour for reading and an hour for writing every day.

As in the chaotic scenario described above with the fire drill and the last-minute speaker, the key to planning is flexibility. One of the best ways to learn about how to plan flexibly is to learn from other teachers, and to hear about how they solve the problems inherent in planning for quality instruction. But teaching tends to be very isolating, with little or no time to truly work with and learn from our colleagues. Since I have become a literacy coordinator, I have been exposed to many incredible teachers, and I have seen them working magic with children. I talked with a few of them about how they meet the challenge of planning for effective writing instruction.

A visit with Chris Hyde, second–grade teacher

I met Chris when I was asked to go to Sunrise Elementary, a year-round school in Cherry Creek District. When I first visited her classroom in the fall, her students were quietly eating snacks and writing in their journals. After about fifteen minutes of sustained writing time, students were invited to share their work with their classmates. Everyone listened carefully and gave specific praise and sound advice as pieces were shared.

I was very impressed with the independence of the students, the quality of their writing, and the higher-order thinking that came out of their discussions. I was anxious to talk to Chris about how she set up this routine.

Early in the year, Chris asks her students to brainstorm ideas for writing based on their own lives. She then types the list of possible topics they could write about and glues it in the front of their journals. The journals become a place for daily writing and a source for pieces that may become final copies.

In another part of the day, Chris introduces students to a writing topic through a mini-lesson, then asks students to write for twenty to thirty minutes, followed by a sharing time. The mini-lesson might be based on a book they have been reading, or it may be introducing a genre of writing. The second graders in her class write personal narratives, expository pieces, poetry, and a research-based nonfiction book during the year, so mini-lesson times are often used to help students understand the features of these genres of writing.

To meet the diverse needs of the students in her class, Chris knows she must form a bond with them first. She wants them to feel comfortable with writing, because she knows if they don't feel confident about their abilities, they won't be able to produce strong writing. Chris is enthusiastic about writing herself, and this obviously translates into the writing her students produce.

Conferences are difficult to manage in primary classrooms, so at times Chris meets with a small group who might have the same need or strength. These small groups can then focus on how to improve their writing, and the discussion can be around one topic. Students who struggle are given a bit more time than other students at the beginning of a writing block if necessary to get them started. More advanced students are encouraged to write more as they are ready, and to explore more complex text structures. Chris is one of those teachers who knows that motivation is a strong component in writing, and if some students are passionate about a particular type of writing that does not fit neatly into a specific genre study, she provides support for these students so that they can explore their passions while she monitors their progress.

Chris has had different schedules during her teaching career, but the year she saw the most growth in writing, she was able to spend approximately one hour and fifteen minutes a day for writing time. Half an hour was set aside for the journal writing and sharing described above, and then forty-five minutes was spent on a mini-lesson, more writing time, and sharing of a particular genre being studied in a class. But time alone is not what creates the growth in Chris' students; it is the way she uses her time that makes the difference.

Roberta Reed and her fourth graders

Like Chris, Roberta knows that the relationship with her students is the key to success in any educational endeavor. She establishes rapport with her students with high expectations for academic assignments and behavior. She has open dialogues with her students about how they can all work together to get better at all subjects, and how to keep a positive attitude.

Roberta, a teacher at Highline Elementary, is not afraid to take risks with her students. She is passionate about writing, and writes in front of her students regularly. Her students listen carefully to her thoughts about writing while she composes on the computer. They watch her change her mind, cross something out or delete it from the screen, and then continue on. Roberta is not afraid to struggle in front of her students. She knows writing is not easy, but she also knows that her students can perform at high levels if they have the right mind-set. Showing them that she gets stuck as a writer, and then demonstrating how she works through the tough spots, helps students believe they, also, can get "unstuck."

Early in the school year, Roberta noticed that her students often struggled with producing high-quality writing. She brought this to their attention, not to make them feel bad, but to brainstorm ways they could work together to improve the situation. She asked them how they might all get better at writing. They suggested that they work on writing for homework. When she asked them if they wanted to choose the topics, they said they would rather have her think of topics to write about. So, for a few months, Roberta assigned a quick-write to her students each night. The topics were focused, but also open-ended: students might write about something fun they liked to do with friends, or they might describe a birthday party or their favorite season. Each day, several students read their writing aloud, and the class listened for examples of strong writing. It didn't take long before all the students' writing improved. They were proud of their efforts, and looked forward to sharing their writing with classmates. I have had the pleasure of visiting Roberta's classroom on several occasions, and they are eager to share their new pieces with me. With Roberta's careful guidance, they have become very strong, motivated writers. I asked Roberta about one student who had made tremendous growth that year, who moved from hating to write to enthusiastically creating strong pieces and then sharing them. I wanted to know what the key to her success was.

"He still hates to write, I think. But he writes because he has a relationship with me."

Having been in Roberta's classroom, I believe she is right. She has created an environment in which all students feel they can write, even if writing is not their favorite subject.

One way that Roberta creates enthusiasm for writing in her

classroom is by reading selected student writing early in the year to the whole class. She reads with such enthusiasm and emotion that soon everyone wants to share their writing. These shared pieces become the basis for noticing things about writing, and the class creates a list of things that they do well. The list becomes a benchmark for all of the students.

Vocabulary development is an important key to Roberta's success in writing. Many of her students are English Language Learners, and some come to her with very little English. She helps to build their vocabulary and their ability to write descriptively by asking them to write lists of adjectives that could describe a common noun. Students can use a dictionary, thesaurus, or each other for this list. Then, once the list is developed, students create a sentence using the noun, a strong verb, and some of the descriptive adjectives. The sentence is illustrated and shared with the class. Roberta finds that this allows her students to build their vocabulary while they are writing, and many of the words begin to show up in students' everyday writing.

Another way that Roberta builds vocabulary is by asking students to memorize a short poem each week. The poem is recited by each student, individually, on Friday. Students build a sense of the rhythms of English with this requirement, and they also build confidence. Even limited English speakers take part in the Friday recitation, and the exercises have definitely paid off: Roberta's students have developed an innate sense of descriptive writing, and it seems to come to them automatically.

Roberta believes that there is value in the quantity of writing students produce. She does not bring too many pieces to final copy, but she provides ample time for modeling her writing, allowing students to practice, and then to share what they have written. They read like writers, using the ideas of Katie Wood Ray. As her students finish a writing piece that Roberta has structured for them, they can go on to freewrite: some students are working on long stories or novels, while others prefer to write poetry in their free time.

Roberta keeps samples of student writing throughout the year, and she will work with these same students next year. The progress she has seen in her students will only continue as they explore the possibilities, with a flexible, master teacher as the guide.

Before she became a fifth-grade teacher, Megan worked as a journalist, so her stories of her days at *Ski* magazine fill her students' imaginations. Megan brings something to her work that many of us cannot: real-world experience as a published writer. When I spoke to her about her beliefs about writing instruction, she first mentioned choice. Though she normally works within a genre of writing with her students, she feels that students can only remain interested in the entire writing process—from first idea, to draft, through revision, to final published piece—if they have some ownership about what they write.

Megan Henry, writer and teacher

She believes strongly that if she assigns writing to her fifth graders, she should complete the assignment as well. She writes with her students, and she is willing to make herself vulnerable so that they can see what the process of writing is all about. She believes that because she is willing to model, her students are not shy about sharing their writing. The community has been created from her willingness to join them in the work.

Due to scheduling constraints, Megan tries to block forty-five minutes per day for writing instruction, but she does not always succeed. It is a testament to her teaching that her students complain when writing time has to be shortened. Megan structures her week by starting with a mini-lesson on Monday or Tuesday based on her students' needs, and then providing time for writing on Wednesday and Thursday. Friday is a day for sharing. She often asks students to just share a portion of their writing until they complete a published piece. This allows more students' voices to be heard, and it also encourages the students because they want to hear more. She may ask students to find their most poetic line to share, and this creates an interest in hearing more from this piece later.

Megan completes genre studies in fiction, memoir, feature articles based on research, and poetry. She never announces to students that she is helping them to get ready for state testing, but rather just infuses her instructional practice with writing that mimics what the state tests often require: various forms of expository writing and narrative writing. Since students in her class work on these genres anyway, she doesn't feel the need to change her instruction dramatically just to get ready for testing time.

For assessment purposes, Megan keeps samples of student work. She looks for and monitors student growth in writing, and she relies on her anecdotal conference notes. These documents help her to determine strengths and weaknesses, and she informs her instruction based on student need. She talks to her writers, and keeps struggling writers close by so that she can encourage them individually during writing time. Megan is a teacher, a writer, and a mentor. Her students benefit from her knowledge of the art of writing and in the art of teaching.

Final thoughts

Chris, Roberta, and Megan embody many of the same ideas in their writing classrooms. They all believe in providing some type of choice for students, they try to get as much time as possible for writing in their classrooms, and they form close relationships with their students. They are also enthusiastic about writing, and this translates into the writing their students produce. I believe that one trait all good teachers share is a passion for what they are teaching. When we care about what we are asking students to do, then students also care. In the writing classroom, we can show our passion by sharing our writing with our students, joining them in the process so that we may all learn together how to put words to our experiences, our hopes, and our dreams. Once we have that passion, the plans will fall into place—not always neatly, and not without interruption, but with a solid foundation from which student writing can flourish.

APPENDIX A

Books to Support Memoir Writing

Moments in time/snapshots

Yolen, J. 1987. *Owl Moon*. New York: Philomel.

A moment in time featuring a young girl hoping to see an owl while walking with her father one snowy night. Works well with all ages.

Rylant, C. 1985. *The Relatives Came*. New York: Simon and Schuster.

Always works for generating stories about relatives visiting, or going to visit relatives.

Brinckloe, J. 1985. *Fireflies*. New York: Simon and Schuster.

Great to help students find stories in their lives about friends in their neighborhood. Features a strong theme in the end.

Rylant, C. 1991. *Night in the Country*. New York: Simon and Schuster.

Perfect for understanding the need to observe the world in which you live. Perfect for helping students write well-crafted sentences about their surroundings.

Baylor, B. 1974. *Everybody Needs a Rock*. New York: Simon and Schuster.

For nature-enthusiasts—helps writers find beauty in the natural world.

Coy, J. 1991. *Night Driving*. New York: Henry Holt.

Excellent story about a boy driving with his father at night to go camping. The story slows down on the journey, giving snapshots of small events along the way.

Crews, D. 1998. *Night at the Fair*. New York: William Morrow & Company, Inc.

Very few words and brilliant pictures capture the excitement of an amusement park. Perfect model for encouraging students to focus in on one event at an amusement park. Illustrations lend themselves to practicing descriptive writing.

Paulsen, G. 1999. *Canoe Days*. New York: Random House.
This text uses beautifully descriptive language to illustrate a love for nature.

Experiences longer than one day

Coy, J. 2003. *Two Old Potatoes and Me*. New York: Random House.
A girl and her father plant potatoes, and wait for them to grow. Interesting visual elements using text, with a great recipe at the end.

Chall, M. W. 1992. *Up North at the Cabin*. New York: William Morrow & Company, Inc.
The perfect book to help students discover how to write about meaningful places in their lives.

Wong, J. S. 2000. *The Trip Back Home*. New York: Harcourt, Inc.
Strong narrative about a girl visiting family in Korea. Excellent source for helping students structure longer stories about travel, or visiting relatives.

Bunting, E. 1996. *Going Home*. New York: Harper Collins.
An immigrant family visits relatives in Mexico—the place the parents call home, but their children think of America as home. A good book for helping students write memoirs about places they visit which may at first resonate more with their parents.

Relationships with grandparents or older people

Joosse, B. M. 2001. *Ghost Wings*. San Francisco: Chronicle Books.
Beautifully written book about a girl's relationship with her grandmother. Though the grandmother dies, the book ends on a very hopeful, uplifting note. The Day of the Dead celebration is described in the book.

Fox, M. 1985. *Wilfrid Gordon MacDonald Partridge*. La Jolla, CA: Kane/Miller Book Publishers.
Classic about a boy who learns about the importance of mem-

ory and friendship. A good source for asking students to bring in artifacts from home to stimulate memoir writing.

Crews, D. 1991. *Bigmama's*. New York: Greenwillow Books.

Visiting relatives, with many anecdotes about family. Excellent as a text for students who are ready to tell about more than just one experience with relatives.

Sports writing

Smith, C. 2001. *Short Takes*. New York: Dutton Children's Books.

Smith, C. 1999. *Rimshots: Basketball Pix, Rolls, and Rhythms*. New York: Penguin.

Charles Smith is a poet and photographer who chronicles his love for basketball. These books are very motivating to students who are interested in sports. Sections of the *Rimshots* book work well as memoir.

APPENDIX B

Books to Support Narrative Writing

Allard, H., and J. Marshall. 1985. *Miss Nelson Has a Field Day.* Boston: Houghton Mifflin.

This book is part of a series in which a teacher's alter ego saves the day in various situations. This is a good text for modeling school stories with a twist.

Anderson, L. H. 2002. *The Big Cheese of Third Street.* New York: Simon and Schuster.

A boy "no bigger than a peanut butter sandwich" (literally) comes to the rescue when his oversized family is challenged in a pole-climbing contest. Great model for adding a fantasy element to the realistic predicament of feeling like a loner in your family.

Birnbaum, A. 1981. *Green Eyes.* Singapore: Golden Books.

Reprint of an older title, a simple tale of a day told through a pet cat's eyes. Provides a model for writing from a pet's point of view.

Brennan, H. 2001. *Frankenstella and the Video Store Monster.* New York: Bloomsbury Children's Books.

A girl whose mother does not believe there is a monster in the video store changes into a Frankenstein-like creature and battles the monster. Hilarious, full of action, and will appeal to kids who like writing hyperbole.

Cronin, D. 2003. *Diary of a Worm.* New York: Harper Collins / Jo-anne Cotler Books.

Days in the life of an average worm. Can be used to spark imaginative writing from an animal's perspective. Very clever, and will appeal to students who like to use facts about animals in creative ways.

Cronin, D. 2000. *Click, Clack, Moo: Cows That Type.* New York: Simon and Schuster.

Cows make demands in a series of letters to a farmer in this hilarious, now classic book. Opportunities abound for students to write their own stories in a series of persuasive letters.

Danneberg, J. 2000. *First Day Jitters*. Watertown, MA: Charlesbridge Publishing.

Someone is nervous about the first day of school in this story with a great twist on the very last page.

Falconer, I. 2003. *Olivia and the Missing Toy*. New York: Simon and Schuster.

The pig with an attitude returns in this tale of Olivia's missing toy. It turns out the dog has torn it apart, and Olivia learns about forgiveness. Check out all the books in the *Olivia* series for smart, funny narratives about the kid in all of us who just can't quite seem to behave.

Keats, E. J. 1968. *A Letter to Amy*. New York: Penguin Putnam.

Keats' work is classic in that it still resonates with children today. This story about a boy who embarrasses himself in front of a girl right when he wants to invite her to a party is full events we all can identify with. Great for generating ideas for realistic fiction.

Palatini, M. 2000. *Bedhead*. New York: Simon and Schuster.

This over-the-top tale of a boy with out of control hair will help young writers recall similar embarrassing moments. The author uses strings of adjectives and verbs to heighten the boy's predicament in a writing style that appeals to kids.

Van Allsburg, C. 1988. *Two Bad Ants*. Boston: Houghton Mifflin.

Van Allsburg's now classic tale of ants who wander away from the colony is excellent for helping students create narratives from unique points of view.

APPENDIX C

Revising My Writing

My name _____

Share numbers 1, 2, and 3 with your group **after** you read your piece out loud.

1. This is what I wrote **before** I did my revision:

2. This is **how I changed my writing** in the revision:

3. I like my new writing better because:

When other students in my group share, I will think about how I can make my own writing better.

Here are **two things** I can try in my writing. I thought about these things while I was meeting with my group:

1.

2.

APPENDIX D

Descriptive Writing Rubric

4 Points
- My word choice is awesome
- I use words that help the reader to see, hear, and feel what is described
- I use interesting words or descriptions instead of just "everyday" words

3 Points
- I could have chosen better words in one section of my writing
- A few of my words help the reader to see, hear, and feel what is described
- I use a few interesting words or descriptions

2 Points
- I need to search for better, stronger words in two or three sections of my writing
- I have one or two words that help the reader to see, hear, and feel what is described
- I need to use more interesting words and descriptions— most of my words are "everyday" words

1 Point
- I need to search for better words for my whole piece
- I need to use words that help the reader see, hear, and feel what is described
- I need to search for words that aren't just "everyday" words

APPENDIX E

Four Point Generic Writing Rubric

4 Content/Org
- I use important details and information
- I do not lose track of my main idea when I add details
- I organize my ideas logically and effectively

4 Style
- My word choice is awesome and my words fit well with my purpose
- I use interesting words and descriptions to make a picture in the reader's mind
- My sentences are not all the same. I use different beginnings and lengths

4 Skills
- Perfect sentence structure, or one or two errors
- Correct punctuation and capitalization
- Spelling is correct, or minor errors do not prevent understanding

3 Content/Org
- I have some important details, but could include more
- Sometimes my writing moves away from idea, or details don't belong
- I need to connect ideas more clearly

3 Style
- My words fit to my purpose
- I use a few interesting words, and in one or two places I make a picture in the reader's mind
- My sentences are correct, but I do not have different sentence beginnings and/or lengths

3 Skills
- I have several errors in some or all of these:
  __sentences __punctuation __capitalization __spelling, but the reader can still understand my writing

2 Content/Org
- I need more details to clearly explain my ideas
- My writing moves away from the main point
- My writing is like a list of ideas with few details

2 Style
- I need to use specific words to more clearly match my purpose for writing
- I need more descriptions to make a picture in the reader's mind
- I have a few sentence errors, or all sentences are the same structure

2 Skills
- Errors in:
  __sentences __punctuation __capitalization and/or spelling slow the reader down several times to determine meaning

1 Content/Org
- I need to add many details
- My writing has no clear purpose or main idea
- My writing is not organized or the ideas are not connected

1 Style
- My words are confusing or unclear
- I need many more descriptions and specific sensory details to make a picture in the reader's mind
- I have a combination of sentence errors and sentence structures are all the same

1 Skills
Many errors in:
__sentences
__punctuation

Totals: Content/Org x 2 = ___   Style x 2 = ___   Skills x 1 = ___   Total Score = ___

Total Score = _____

1 2 3 4 5 6	= Unsatisfactory	A = 18, 19, 20
7 8 9 10 11 12 13 14	= Partially Proficient	B = 16, 17
15 16 17 18	= Proficient	C = 14, 15
19 20	= Advanced	D = 11, 12, 13

APPENDIX F

Yearlong Plan: Fifth Grade

September	October	November
Units of Study:		
Memoir (3 wks)	Narrative (3 wks)	Compare/contrast essay
Technical writing	Description (ongoing)	(in social studies) (1 week)
(in science) (4 wks)		Persuasive writing (2 wks)
Description (ongoing)		

Poetry (2 to 3 times per month until April)
Prompt practice (2 times per month until March)

Deadlines: (pieces indicated are best efforts, chosen by students)

1 memoir	1 story	1 essay comparing colonial times
1 science fair project	2 descriptive pieces	with our times
1 prompt practice	1 prompt practice	1 descriptive piece
1 poem	poem	1 persuasive piece
	1	1 poem

December	January	February
Units of Study:		
Publishing (2 wks)	Research (4 wks)	Narrative (2 wks)
(3 pieces revisited for publication)	Writing to explain(in science)	Summaries (in social studies)

Poetry (2 to 3 times per month until April)
Prompt practice (2 times per month until March)

Deadlines:

3 published pieces	1 research project	1 story
1 prompt practice	1 explanatory piece	2 summaries
1 poem	1 prompt practice	1 prompt practice
	1 poem	1 poem

March	April	May
Units of Study:		
Publish book of poetry	Me Magazine (6 wks)	Me Magazine (publishing)
Research (in social studies) (3 wks)	Persuasive (in science) (2 wks)	

Poetry (2 to 3 times per month until April)
Prompt practice (2 times per month until March)

Deadlines:

Poetry book	1 persuasive piece	1 magazine
1 research project		

APPENDIX G

Recommended Books by Topic

Setting up a writer's workshop, grades 3 and up

Chancer, J., and G. Rester-Zodrow. 1997. *Moon Journals: Writing, Art, and Inquiry*. Portsmouth, NH: Heinemann.

Davis, J., and S. Hill. 2003. *The No-Nonsense Guide to Teaching Writing: Strategies, Structures, and Solutions*. Portsmouth, NH: Heinemann.

Ray, K. W. 2001. *The Writing Workshop: Working Through the Hard Parts (And They're All Hard Parts)*. Urbana, IL: National Council of Teachers of English.

Routman, R. 2004. *Writing Essentials: Raising Expectations and Results While Simplifying Teaching*. Portsmouth, NH: Heinemann.

Teaching Writing in the Primary Grades

Calkins, L. 2003. *Units of Study for Primary Writing: A Yearlong Curriculum (K–2)*. Portsmouth, NH.

Cleveland, L., and K. W. Ray. 2004. *About the Authors: Writing Workshop with Our Youngest Writers*. Portsmouth, NH: Heinemann.

Stead, T. 2002. *Is That a Fact? Teaching Nonfiction Writing K–3*. Portland, ME: Stenhouse.

Revising

Heard, G. 2002. *The Revision Toolbox: Teaching Techniques That Work*. Portsmouth, NH: Heinemann.

Lane, B. 1999. *The Reviser's Toolbox*. Shoreham, VT: Discover Writing Press.

Poetry

Flynn, N., and S. McPhillips. 2000. *A Note Slipped Under the Door: Teaching from Poems We Love*. Portland, ME: Stenhouse.

Heard, G. 1999. *Awakening the Heart; Exploring Poetry in Elementary and Middle School.* Portsmouth, NH: Heinemann.

Lies, B. B. 1993. *The Poet's Pen: Writing Poetry with Middle and High School Students.* Teacher Ideas Press.

Prompt Practice for Test Preparation

Schaefer, L. M. 2002. *10 Writing Lessons for the Overhead.* New York: Scholastic.

References

Allen, J. 2004. *Tools for Teaching Content Literacy.* Portland, ME: Stenhouse Publishers.

Anderson, C. 2000. *How's It Going? A Practical Guide to Conferring with Student Writers.* Portsmouth, NH: Heinemann.

Atwell, N. 1998. *In the Middle: New Understandings About Writing, Reading, and Learning.* Portsmouth, NH: Boynton/Cook Publishers, Inc.

Brinckloe, J. 1985. *Fireflies.* New York: Simon and Schuster.

Buehl, D. 2001. *Classroom Strategies for Interactive Learning.* 2d ed. Newark, DE: International Reading Association.

Calkins, L. 2003. *Units of Study for Primary Writing: A Yearlong Curriculum (K–2).* Portsmouth, NH: Heinemann.

Calkins, L. 1986. *The Art of Teaching Writing.* Portsmouth, NH: Heinemann.

Daniels, H. 2002. *Literature Circles.* Portland, ME: Stenhouse Publishers.

DiCamillo, K. 2000. *Because of Winn-Dixie.* Cambridge, MA: Candlewick Press.

Fletcher, R. 1992. *What a Writer Needs.* Portsmouth, NH: Heinemann.

Graves, D. 1982. *Writing: Teachers and Children at Work.* Portsmouth, NH: Heinemann.

Harvey, S., and A. Goudvis. 2000. *Strategies That Work.* Portland, ME: Stenhouse Publishers.

Heard, G. 1999. *Awakening the Heart: Exploring Poetry in Elementary and Middle School.* Portsmouth, NH: Heinemann.

Loebel, A. 1979. *Days with Frog and Toad.* New York: Harper Collins Publishers.

Macrorie, K. 1985. *Telling Writing.* Portsmouth, NH: Boynton/Cook.

Murray, D. M. 1985. *A Writer Teaches Writing: A Complete Revision.* Boston: Houghton-Mifflin.

Ray, K. W. 1999. *Wondrous Words.* IL: National Council of Teachers of English.

Ringgold, F. 1991. *Tar Beach*. New York: Crown Publishers.

Sachar, L. 1998. *Holes*. New York: Random House.

———. 1978. *Sideways Stories from Wayside School*. New York: Harper Trophy.

Santa, C. 1988. *Content Reading Including Study Systems*. Dubuque, IA: Kendall/Hunt.

Santa, C., L. Havens, and S. Harrison. 1989. "Teaching Secondary Science Through Reading, Writing, Studying, and Problem Solving." In D. Lapp, J. Flood, and N. Farnan, eds., *Content-Area Reading and Learning: Instructional Strategies*. Englewood Cliffs, NJ: Prentice-Hall.

Teague, M. 2004. *Detective LaRue*. New York: Scholastic.

———. 2002. *Dear Mrs. LaRue*. New York: Scholastic.

Van Allsburg, C. 1996. *The Mysteries of Harris Burdick: The Portfolio Edition (posters)*. New York: Houghton Mifflin.

———. 1984. *The Mysteries of Harris Burdick*. New York: Houghton Mifflin.

Wallace, K. 1998. *Gentle Giant Octopus*. Cambridge, MA: Candlewick Press.

Weaver, C. 1996. *Teaching Grammar in Context*. Portsmouth, NH: Boynton Cook Publishers.

Weisner, D. 1991. *Tuesday*. New York: Houghton Mifflin.

Worth, V. 1994. *All the Small Poems*. New York: Farrar, Straus, Giroux.

Yolen, J. 1987. *Owl Moon*. New York: Scholastic.